# Turned On
## and
# Tuned Out

*A Practical Guide to Understanding
and Managing Tech Dependence*

JOHN K. KRIGER

WESTBOW°
PRESS
A DIVISION OF THOMAS NELSON
& ZONDERVAN

WestBow Press books may be ordered through booksellers or by contacting:

WestBow Press
A Division of Thomas Nelson & Zondervan
1663 Liberty Drive
Bloomington, IN 47403
www.westbowpress.com
1 (866) 928-1240

ISBN: 978-1-4908-3512-9 (sc)
ISBN: 978-1-4908-3513-6 (hc)
ISBN: 978-1-4908-3511-2 (e)

Library of Congress Control Number: 2014907862

Printed in the United States of America.

WestBow Press rev. date: 05/22/2014

# Contents

To my wife Yvette, the secret to any success I've enjoyed in my life and whose encouragement and support allowed me to accomplish anything close to this or many of the other successes I enjoy.

# Acknowledgments

Thank you to all of those individuals who helped me make this book a reality. My wife has taught me the value of taking action on things I believe in and completing what I start. Watching her consistent and sustained passion for helping others, I have found a greater meaning in my own life and the motivation for this book. With her steady guidance and continued input, I've been able to realize and learn far more than I could ever have accomplished on my own. There is no one I know who gives more of herself, leaving me with no doubt that this world is infinitely better because she is in my life. As my partner and friend, I have watched her give totally of herself to friends, family, and our children to the point of self-sacrifice. She has taught me balance in my life and a greater faith in God, and I am certain that, without her, I would be far less than who I am today.

Thanks to our kids, Bryan, Megan, Gen, and Sam, and our sons-in-law, Kyle and Brent, who all constantly provided me with material to think about as well as their own experiences and insights.

Pat Iyer, thank you for your encouragement, editing, and feedback. Your strong and steady support over the past several years means more than you will ever know. Thanks to Brian Eckenhoff for your editing and attention to the flow of this document. Special thanks to Samantha Kriger. Your final edits and sound guidance on the details helped me to put this book together with attention to details that I would have never seen.

I also want to thank the thousands of individuals who have attended and unselfishly shared their own stories at my seminars, lectures, and classes. I only pray that the information I have learned and shared here and in my sessions is provided with care, respect, and integrity to honor your experiences. I sincerely appreciate all of your help, guidance, and assistance.

# Preface

Let's face it. Technology is everywhere. Today, you would have difficulty functioning without it. From the moment you wake up, technology dominates your days. From your alarm clock to the alarm system you may set before leaving the house to the car you drive and even to the machines you use at work, technology is everywhere!

We have all advanced as a world through the innovation and amazing capacity of technology. I'm sure even Bill Gates didn't fully envision the impact technology would have on individuals' day-to-day lives. The impact, capacity, and potential of technology today is almost incomparable to anything else. Technology has almost unlimited potential. However, whether or not that potential is positive or negative largely depends on the individual's behavior and the influence of the environment in which he lives and works.

This guide provides you with the information necessary to examine and evaluate your own technology use. If you have children, it will give insight into potential hazards and what you can do to offset them. It will help you determine if your home and/or work environments help to create healthy settings from which you and others can appropriately and beneficially interact with today's technology.

As you read through the material in this guide, look at the potential impact that technology can have on you, your families, the workplace, and society at large. Consider the prevalence of technology in your life and your family as we raise some important questions about the appropriate use of a variety of technological tools.

This guide discusses in detail the signs and stages of both technology abuse and technology dependence. Unhealthy technology use—much like the abuse of drugs or alcohol—begins with abuse and can easily and subtly transition into dependence. The guide provides you with helpful tips and strategies for monitoring and controlling your own technology use.

These tips will help you and others in your life identify if it is a problem and then assist you to regain control of your technology use to reconnect. Technology has many amazing and wonderful uses, and this manual exists to help you evaluate your usage of technology so you can maintain a healthier and balanced life.

Currently, I have the pleasure of traveling around the country, meeting wonderful people, hearing lots of stories, and providing training programs on various aspects of technology dependence. With my background in behavioral science and addictions, I began seeing a direct correlation between technology dependence and drugs or alcohol years ago, and new research is now validating my observations. With the publishing and release of the *2013 Diagnostic and Statistical Manual V* by the American Psychiatric Association, I was expecting that technology dependence criteria would be recognized as a significant enough behavioral or psychological disorder to be included for diagnostic purposes. As with many other disorders, if it is recognized, prevented, and/or managed, those impacted can find ways to reduce or eliminate the negative impact on their lives. However, I was disappointed. And yet, almost daily I hear of the negative impact technology is having on the lives of individuals and families, and feel it is only a matter of time.

Given its existence with the positives and negatives of its use, if we can assist you or your organization by providing information, consulting, or training regarding the abuse or dependence on technology, please contact us. Be well!

John K. Kriger
President, Kriger Consulting
609-387-5226
info@krigerconsulting.com

# 1

# Do You Remember Your First Computer?

I don't know about you, but I can remember getting my first computer, a Tandy T-1000 from RadioShack. When I got it, my excitement was almost unbearable. I brought it home in multiple large boxes, which required me to put down all the seats in my minivan so I could fit them all in. I needed a hand truck to bring the boxes into the house, and it took both my wife and me just to get it down the flight of stairs into the basement.

Among the boxes and packing material, I stood in my back office, elated by the prospect of entering the digital age. I unpacked the numerous pieces of equipment, cords, and all of the manuals required to set up the computer. After nearly five hours of reading manuals, plugging and unplugging, getting frustrated, and muttering words I won't repeat here, I had set it up at last.

When I first turned on the computer, only a slight hum emitted from the central processing unit. Then a strange and eerie glow appeared as the grayish-black screen lit up with a greenish-gray light, and a small dot began to bounce on the screen. At the time, I'm sure I had no idea my life would be forever changed because of the technology I had brought into my home that day.

For anyone over the age of thirty-five, the pace at which technology has advanced over the past twenty years is almost unfathomable. But for those who are younger than that, working with technology often seems like second nature because you've grown up with these leaps in technology. What used to take hours to set up and learn to use now can be accomplished in minutes and often entails a device no bigger than a deck of cards. The intuitive nature of today's technology has drastically increased not only its capabilities but ultimately the enjoyment of using it. You simply pull out your laptop or cell phone and use it.

Technology continues to evolve at a dizzying pace. Many schools and business now use SMART boards instead of chalk or whiteboards. Flat-screen and three-dimensional TVs are replacing bulky ones, much like color TVs replaced black-and-white ones in the 1950s and 1960s.

The Segway, which only a few years ago was seen as a transportation marvel, has become commonplace in factories, malls, and parks. Glasses and even contact lenses with computer screens set in the lenses are being produced so you can be always connected, hands-free and voice-controlled. The innovations are amazing!

While owning a computer was a luxury the day I brought home my Tandy, most individuals today own not only a cell phone but also a desktop computer, laptop, gaming console, tablet computer, and/or e-reader. In fact, most Americans today have at least one computer in their home. iPods, iPads, and BlackBerrys with the memory and capacity to surpass many desktops are readily available, and a library full of information is now available at the touch of a button from your home or office. In fact, by the time this book is published, many of the current innovations will already be outdated.

Even the most basic access to information today is far greater than anyone could have ever imagined only twenty-five years ago. Concepts spread virally, circling the globe multiple times a day. At no time in history has so much information been this accessible to this many people so quickly. There is more information available to us today without leaving our homes than was ever available to our grandparents throughout the span of their entire lives.

# 2

# Can You Have Too Much of a Good Thing?

> Too much of a good thing is a good thing.
>
> —Kenny Chesney

Thanksgiving at my house has historically been a time when the kids come home and the family gets together to renew our relationships, poke fun at each other, watch some football, and eat far too much food. Every year, we promise to keep our turkey dinner indulgences in moderation. We snack throughout the day to hold out for the big meal to come. But dinner inevitably comes, and we are all far too hungry. We attack the table like ravenous sharks in a feeding frenzy rivaling reality TV until we finally surrender for fear of exploding. Then we use our remaining energy to drag ourselves into the living room, where we unwillingly surrender to a turkey coma, all but unable to move.

I exaggerate to make a point, but I am sure most of you know how easy it is to overindulge in eating, drinking, gambling, shopping, and doing so many other things that we enjoy. When you do anything to the extent that it starts throwing your life out of balance, it's no longer a good thing. And with today's technology, some individuals find it extremely difficult to balance their lives between cyberspace and reality. Research from South Korea says that ten heart-related deaths occurred in 2007 in cybercafés. These individuals reportedly stayed at the computer terminals without taking breaks to eat or drink, physically pushing themselves until they died.

Compulsive video game playing has become a national problem, and it's no coincidence that South Korea considers technology addiction to be one of the primary health issues facing the country.[1] In fact, the average South Korean high school student spends as many as twenty-three hours per week gaming.[2] In China, an estimated 13.7 percent of adolescents who actively use the Internet meet the criteria for technology addiction.[3] As a result, laws are currently being developed to discourage computer usage in excess of three hours per day.[4]

Many Asian countries use cybercafés, rendering the tracking of user numbers much easier than in the United States. In this

---

[1] YH Choi, "Advancement of IT and Seriousness of Youth Internet Addiction," International Symposium on the Counseling and Treatment of Youth Internet Addiction (2007), 20.

[2] BN Kim, "From Internet to "Family-net": Internet Addict vs. Digital Leader," International Symposium on the Counseling and Treatment of Youth Internet Addiction (2007), 196.

[3] S. K. Young, Internet Addiction: A Handbook and Guide to Evaluation and Treatment (Hoboken: John Wiley and Sons, Inc., 2011), 5. http://www.amazon.com/Internet-Addiction-Handbook-Evaluation-Treatment/dp/047055116X

[4] "The More They Play, The More They Lose," accessed April 22, 2013, *People's Daily Online.* http://english.people.com.cn/200704/10/eng20070410_364977.html

country, online games, virtual relationships, gambling, drug sales, and many other addictive behaviors are brought into our homes, offices, dorm rooms, and related places. With our isolated use of technology, the ability to measure the number of individuals affected by technology addiction in the United States is almost impossible.

Individuals use technology daily as they use a computer to complete work, send emails, or play games, use a cell phone to send text messages, and interact with each other through technology. Interpersonal relationships are maintained via videoconferencing, and a highly valued education is now but a click away. Students can notify parents of a delay in the end of a sports practice, while parents can feel assured that their children can reach them in a time of need.

But while technology is a wonderful resource and tool, it is also a detrimental crutch for many. Technology has the potential to suck us into patterns of compulsive usage, impacting us in ways that may prove to be more harmful than beneficial. A January 2011 issue of the *Daily Mail* reported that "we were not just seeing psychological symptoms, but also physical symptoms" in regards to technology addiction, including feelings of anxiousness, increased blood pressure, racing thoughts, and isolation.[5]

Years ago, a fight or misunderstanding at home would be left at home. Phone calls to work were generally for emergency purposes only, and many secretaries or office assistants would not

---

[5] "Technology Junkies: How We Suffer Withdrawal Symptoms like Drug Addicts If We're Kept Away from Our Gadgets," accessed April 22, 2013, *MailOnline.* http://www.dailymail.co.uk/sciencetech/article-1344723/How-suffer-withdrawal-symptoms-like-drug-addicts-kept-away-tech-gadgets.html

put phone calls through if they were of a personal nature. Today though, everyone has personal and often work cell phones with text messaging. This allows personal matters to intrude into the workplace, potentially impacting workers' ability to satisfactorily perform their jobs and pay attention to related tasks while also negatively impacting service to customers and clients.

A man I once interviewed told me about how, when he went to the dentist for a routine checkup, he stood waiting at the check-in window while the receptionist finished typing a text message. He had to wait for a second person in the office to realize he was standing there. The receptionist was so busy texting that she was oblivious to the people and responsibilities around her.

Once while standing in line at my bank, I experienced a similar situation. The person in front of me became engrossed in his text messaging. When he was next in line, I had to tap him on the shoulder to let him know he could move forward, drawing many laughs, coughs, and remarks from those behind me.

As we go forward in this book, we'll discuss the impact of technology on various individuals and systems. As we look into the problems associated with tech abuse and dependence, I believe you will see how our lives are at times completely out of balance as a result of our technology use. Numerous individuals may find that technology interferes with their work, hinders their personal lives, and even creates financial and/or personal hardship. Some individuals even experience physical problems.

And whether you're interested in the effects of technology because of your own level of use or that of someone you know, I'd like you to be open to the possibility that just about anything can be harmful if it throws your life out of balance.

# 3

# Technology Addiction?

Technology abuse and dependence appear to impact the individuals' lives and behaviors much like other addictions. For comparison, we'll look at technology use through the criteria for substance use disorder. If these descriptions fit your technological habits, I provide practical steps to aid you in regaining your lost balance. If the criteria don't seem to fit your habits, you will probably be able to think of at least one person for whom they do. Consider those who could benefit from what you read here. After all, balance provides us with a sense of serenity, effectiveness, and satisfaction.

Numerous measurements in the addictions field determine if someone has a drug or alcohol problem. We'll look at the criteria for substance use disorders, which is based on the *Diagnostic Statistical Manual* (DSM V) that mental health and health-care professionals use to diagnose behavioral and psychological disorders.[6] We'll then examine the substance use disorder criteria

---

[6] American Psychiatric Association. *Diagnostic And Statistical Manual Of Mental Disorders*, 5th ed. (Washington, DC: American Psychiatric Association, 2013). http://www.amazon.com/Diagnostic -Statistical-Disorders-Revision-DSM-IV-TR/dp/0890420254

and the way it relates to the use of technology by looking at the continuum of tech abuse potentially leading into dependence.

The DSM V outlines eleven elements of substance use disorder. Legal issues, which were eliminated from the DSM V, are maintained in this list from the prior DSM IV, while craving, which was added in the new edition is discussed throughout this text. The elements are provided in a somewhat progressive order and in further detail in this chapter:

- failure to fulfill major roles
- use in physically hazardous situations
- use resulting in legal problems
- use resulting in social or interpersonal problems
- tolerance – an increased desire to use more
- withdrawl symptoms
- longer periods of use than intended
- feeling the need to cut down
- spending time using and then recovering from the use
- being less socially, occupationally, or recreationally involved
- continued use, even when it causes problems

It's important to remember that not everyone who uses substances abuses them, just as not everyone who abuses substances goes on to become dependent. But dependency starts with use which can lead to abuse. Like substances, technology use ranges on a continuum from mild to severe. For the purposes of this comparison, we'll substitute the use of technology for the abuse and dependence of a substance.

## Criterion #1: Failure to Fulfill Major Roles

Tech abuse often begins with the failure to fulfill major roles. The choice of technology over significant personal obligations can result in the failure to complete or attend to personal responsibilities. The following are some important questions regarding this stage of tech abuse:

- Have you ever missed important phone calls, events, meetings, or time with your kids because of your texting, talking on the phone, or computer use?
- Have you been late for or missed an important meeting, class, or event because of your technology use?
- Did you ever use work computers to access restricted sites that could cost you your job?

A social worker recently told me of a family where the mother's online activities led to a debate within their offices as to whether the children should be removed from the home due to her neglectful behavior. The mother's online compulsion with FarmVille jeopardized her ability to care for her children and to function in her job as a parent. This mother is now seeking psychological help to reduce her compulsive use of FarmVille in addition to counseling to correct her financial problems from online purchases of virtual livestock and farm equipment.

In another instance, I interviewed a small business owner following a visit to her office by a tech services representative. It seems the owner relieved her secretary of her duties when the secretary complained about several games being removed from her work computer during the computer repairs. The secretary was not fulfilling her job obligations and was not approved to use a business computer for personal use. As a result of her tech abuse, she was relieved of her duties. In addition to lack of approval, her online gaming potentially opened her employer's computers to viruses and malware.

In another conversation with a college administrator, I learned of a West Coast college student who withdrew at the end of his third year because his class schedule was interfering with his World of Warcraft gaming sessions. In spite of his almost 4.0 grade point average, he decided college was not important to him anymore as he was beginning to receive corporate sponsorships to play games at gaming events around the world and be the face of online product sales to other World of Warcraft gamers. While this example is extreme, many students and young adults play computer games until the early hours of the morning and are unable to function at school, if they even make it to class the next day.

Excess gaming isn't limited to students, though. In some cases, workers spend hours playing games well into the early hours of the next morning and, as a result, can barely function on the assembly line or in the office the next day. In both instances, many have told me how often they require a caffeine boost or energy drink to give them the energy they need to function after spending half the night playing video or online games.

When individuals push their limits without adequate rest or hydration, while continuing to abuse themselves with caffeine and other stimulants, a lengthy period of recovery is often necessary. This negatively impacts their ability to function and to fulfill their major role as a parent, partner, employee, or student. Adequate rest is required to be attentive at work or in class and to be able to focus for any period of time.

## Criterion #2: Use in Physically Hazardous Situations

Think back to any situation that may have been physically hazardous to yourself or others that occurred while you were using technology. Here are some helpful questions to help you think through for the second criterion of tech abuse:

- While driving, have you ever found yourself drifting into another lane because you were using your cell phone, texting, or programming your GPS?
- Have you ever been looking something up or texting only to discover yourself coming up quickly on a tollbooth or about to miss a traffic signal?
- Or have you witnessed others driving or even walking with headphones on, oblivious of the world around them?

I'm sure you can pinpoint a time where some type of technology significantly distracted you or someone you know. I witnessed this daily on secondary highways, as well as at seventy miles an hour on the New Jersey Turnpike. Two days before I wrote this, I witnessed a woman driving a Lamborghini sports car at about eighty miles an hour with her cell phone positioned in both hands at the top of the steering wheel while taking pictures or texting as she drove! She crossed the dividing lines numerous times, totally oblivious of the traffic around her.

When I first started using a cell phone, I know I found myself enamored with it. One day, I was driving and trying to look up a number when I suddenly found myself headed directly toward a tollbooth because I was distracted. Did it impair my driving? You bet! Was I putting others at risk? Certainly!

In fact, according to a 2006 University of Utah study, "motorists who talk on handheld or hands-free cellular phones are as impaired as drunken drivers."[7] And as a result, I have all but stopped using my phone (even hands-free) while driving. Realistically, there are times when using the phone while driving may be necessary, but these events are rare. And even without my own use, I can't tell you how many close calls I've had on the Turnpike because of someone else driving extremely slow, weaving across lanes, or even almost rear-ending me because she is on a cell phone.

If we are willing to engage in a behavior, then we also need to be able to accept the responsibility for anything that could happen because of that behavior. No one is perfect, but we sure can minimize the risk involved to ourselves and others by merely waiting until we find a rest stop to use our electronic devices or pulling off the road to avoid injuring ourselves or those around us. If you can't control yourself not to answer that text message or phone call, put the phone in the trunk of your car before you set out. Reduce your temptation. It's not worth dying over!

---

[7] "Drivers on Cell Phones Are as Bad as Drunks," accessed April 22, 2013, *News Center: The University of Utah*. http://unews.utah.edu/old/p/062206-1.html

Here are some alarming statistics from the National Highway Traffic Safety Administration regarding distracted driving:[8]

- 18 percent of all injury-related crashes in 2010 were directly related to distracted driving.
- 40 percent of all American teens say they have been in a car when the driver used a cell phone in a way that put people in danger.
- Text messaging creates a crash risk twenty-three times worse than driving while not distracted.

Our willingness to use technology in these physically hazardous situations reveals some level of tech abuse in our lives. And driving while using technology presents a tremendous liability to businesses and accounts for impairment equal to someone with a blood alcohol content (BAC) of .08 percent, not taking into account the impact to the family of the person arrested, injured, or owning the business.

It is now a routine practice as part of accident investigations for law enforcement, lawyers, and the courts to review phone records for indications of texting or phone use at the time of an accident. Both the time of the use and content can be reviewed, resulting in substantial consequences. State legislatures are developing additional legislation allowing enforcement officers to confiscate cell phones to determine if the phone were being use at the time of the accident.

---

[8] "What Is Distracted Driving?" accessed June 10, 2013, distraction.gov. http://www.distraction.gov/content/get-the-facts/facts-and-statistics.html

## Criterion #3: Use Resulting in Legal Problems

Most individuals who use technology do not have legal complications. However, many people have put themselves at risk through their use of their phone, computer, or the Internet.

Have you ever misused your computer during work time to shop, play games, send personal e-mails, or do other non-work related activities? If you've done this without the permission of your employer, this is legally considered theft of time and unauthorized use. Most of us don't think anything of taking a few minutes periodically to send a private email or to look up some fact, trivia, or bit of information we need to fulfill our personal lives.

While most of this behavior is benign, many of these personal actions, which appear to be innocent acts, could put your workplace and your job in jeopardy. Many organizations today track personal use of phones, computers, and the Internet because they recognize the immense liability and cost to the business.

Many individuals do not recognize that personal use of a company mobile phone for texting or sending email gives the business the legal right to use all of those communications against you should they choose to. For individuals abusing technology, their technological habits put them in jeopardy for legal consequences as a result.

## Criterion #4: Use Resulting in Social or Interpersonal Problems

Like substances, technology use ranges on a continuum from mild to severe and from functional use to dependence. Here are some helpful questions at this stage of the discussion on tech abuse:

- Do you tend to avoid people in favor of spending time with your technology?
- Are you experiencing less and less offline social contact?
- Do you have increasing difficulty picking up on social cues when you do spend time with others?
- Are you growing more impatient, finishing others' sentences, or becoming annoyed when someone doesn't respond as quickly as you'd like?

As we spend more and more time with technology, we experience less and less interpersonal interaction. A priest recently told me of two annulments he was involved in. One was because of online gambling; the other was due to compulsive viewing of pornography. Unfortunately, these stories weren't the first I've heard like them. In fact, I am constantly hearing of marriages and relationships deteriorating due to one partner's time being spent on the Internet rather than building the relationship.

A relationship, whether professional or personal in nature, needs to be nurtured. Without investing the time to cultivate understanding and learning to trust through basic social interactions, we miss developing a level of intimacy and integrity, which can only be built over time. Every time we choose email over face-to-face meetings, we miss out on an opportunity to further develop a relationship. The ability to develop relationships worsens as our number of face-to-face interactions decrease.

A parent I recently met at one of my tech addiction presentations told me that she and her daughter rarely speak to each other in full sentences anymore. Instead, they speak primarily in text language! Other parents tell me they no longer yell to their kids that dinner is ready or that they are ready to leave. They now just text them because that is the only thing they immediately react to.

During one of our seminars, a woman complained because her sister no longer takes phone calls. "If you want to get in contact with her, you either have to text her or send her an email," she said. "She no longer takes phone calls or unscheduled visits." Instead, they have reduced their communication to text language, as they feel this is a more efficient use of their time.

Texting and emailing are excellent forms of communications for distributing facts, figures, and exchanging brief and relatively basic information. However, text and email totally miss the nuances of speech, facial expression, and body language that provide context in face-to-face communication.

Interpersonal relationships and social interactions often suffer because of the use of and overreliance on technology. This is a good indicator that we have strayed from functional technological use into technology abuse.

The material in this chapter serves to provide you the tools necessary to evaluate your technology use. I challenge you to sincerely and genuinely interact with the material and questions provided to examine where you might stand along the dysfunction technological spectrum.

As a reminder, each of the criteria being presented builds upon one another in terms of increasing reliance upon technology. Individuals may not show signs of all the criteria at the same time, but each successive criterion signals deepening overreliance and potentially dependence.

## Criterion #5: Tolerance – An Increased Desire to Use More

Do you remember when you first began using the computer, when you would feel stiff and sore after sitting for extended periods of time? Often your eyes would get tired, and you would need to get up and stretch. Over time though, you began to develop the ability to sit for longer periods of time, take fewer breaks, and focus for longer periods of time. Essentially, we have conditioned our bodies to develop a tolerance for longer and longer periods of time at the computer or in front of the TV.

According to a study by the Kaiser Family Foundation, eight- to eighteen-year-olds spend around seven and a half hours viewing entertainment media on any given day.[9] This equals almost fifty-three hours per week. In a 2008 study funded by the National

---

[9] The Henry J. Kaiser Family Foundation, "Daily Media Use among Children and Teens Up Dramatically from Five Years Ago," accessed April 22, 2013. http://kff.org/disparities-policy/press-release/daily-media-use-among-children-and-teens-up-dramatically-from-five-years-ago/

Cancer Institute of Canada and the Canadian Cancer Society, research found the following:[10]

- Most teenagers (60 percent) spend an average of twenty hours a week in front of television and/or computer screens.
- One-third of all teenagers spend closer to forty hours a week in front of technology screens.
- About 7 percent of teens are exposed to more than fifty hours a week of screen time.

In some cases, individuals are spending over forty-eight and a half hours per week playing video games.[11] That is more than a full-time job!

What does all this mean for the development and maintenance of the interpersonal skills that teens and adults will need in life to work in teams, get their needs met effectively, and involve themselves in groups and interpersonal relationships? Behaviors repeated consistently over time tend to become habitual. The more you practice, the better you become at whatever you do. On the flip side, ignoring a learned skill or ability causes it to fade or be reduced from what it could have been. Buy a house plant, and don't water it. Or ignore your relationships for an extended period. Observe the results. Whatever you pay attention to tends

---

[10] "Many Teens Spend 30 Hours A Week On 'Screen Time' During High School," accessed April 22, 2013, *ScienceDaily*. http://www.sciencedaily.com/releases/2008/03/080312172614.htm

[11] "Extreme Gamers Spend Two Full Days Per Week Playing Video Games," accessed April 22, 2013, *NPD Group: Behind Every Business Decision*. https://www.npd.com/wps/portal/npd/us/news/press-releases/pr_100527b/

to become more firmly embedded in your behavior and your brain, and the rest starts to wither. The more we spend time building a tolerance for screen time, the more we neglect our personal relationships and their further development.

## Criterion #6: Withdrawal Symptoms

When responsible individuals attempt to limit access to cell phones or computers, they are often faced with a displeased, if not violent, response. One parent I was speaking with recently told me that her usually very well behaved sixteen-year-old daughter threw an all-out temper tantrum when her phone and texting privileges were removed because of inappropriate use. A crisis counselor told me of a situation where the parents of a fifteen-year-old male, a good student with no prior history of behavioral problems, took the computer away from their son because he played a particular online video game after he had told them he was going to bed.

Early into the morning, his father got up to find him still playing. When this young man was told his computer was off limits for a week, he became enraged and began punching holes in the hallway of his home and trashing his room. Despite attempts by his parents to calm him from outside of his locked bedroom door, it was not until the police were called that they found he had punched holes in his bedroom walls and basically destroyed his room. He was subsequently taken to a psychiatric facility for evaluation. The mere restriction of his computer caused him to come undone.

Many of the individuals in my coaching and training sessions report feeling extremely anxious without their electronic devices.

Many users indicate that they will go to great lengths to retrieve a cell phone or tablet computer left at home.

When I visited my local car dealership for an oil change, their business was completely shut down when a transformer behind their building shorted out, cutting off all of their electricity. Workers reported that customers were extremely understanding, while their coworkers on the other hand were frustrated, irritated, and angry because of the loss of computer access.

Parents tell me that taking away a cell phone or video games has resulted in family violence, running away, and injury of family members.

## Criterion #7: Longer Periods of Use Than Intended

"I'll be right down in a minute!" he called down to his wife. Thirty-five minutes later, she climbed the stairs only to find him still on the computer. Sound familiar?

This scenario is played out daily with adults and children, women and men, and teens and seniors all losing track of time consumed by the interactive and seductive nature of technology. Meetings are often delayed and deadlines missed because individuals get tied up in their own techno world. Have you ever lost track of time playing Solitaire, FarmVille, Bejeweled Blitz, Candy Crush, or other computer games or significantly underestimated just how long you were on your cell phone?

In one case, three nurses were reportedly fired because of their lack of awareness regarding just how long they were on a popular social networking site. Engrossed in this popular site, they failed to notice a patient who had pushed his help button.

Growing frustrated when his call for assistance went unanswered, he attempted to get up from his hospital bed and fell, hitting his head. The patient sustained a fatal blow to the skull, and the nurses weren't even aware he had fallen. The union is reportedly having a very difficult time in defending the nurses' actions, and their dismissal was anticipated as being imminent.

## Criterion #8: Feeling the Need to Cut Down

I am aware of several child neglect cases being considered for the removal of children from their homes due to the single parent playing FarmVille and other computer games. Even those in the technology field are beginning to recognize that some aspects of our tech use may be out of balance. In a CNN Tech report, Steve Wozniak, co-founder of Apple Computer stated, "All of a sudden, we've lost a lot of control. We can't turn off our Internet; we can't turn off our Smartphones; we can't turn off our computers."[12]

As we become increasingly dependent on technology, we may find that it is starting to control our lives. Many times, we react by trying to control the very thing that is controlling us. During one of my training sessions, a therapist reported seeing more than one client working to control his or her excessive computer game use. Her clients reportedly feel guilty and out of control, spending money meant for their children instead on equipment and animals for FarmVille.

---

[12] Mark Milan, "Apple's Steve Wozniak: 'We've lost a lot of control,'" accessed April 22, 2013, CNN Tech. http://www.cnn.com/2010/TECH/innovation/12/08/steve.wozniak.computers/

Compulsive gambling, pornography, phone or computer sex, excessive gaming, and even electronic tones that change brain function by replicating the effects of drug use are becoming commonplace. So are the denial, guilt, anger, frustration, and pain associated with increased trying to control an area of addictive dependence.

## Criterion #9: Spending Time Using and Then Recovering From the Use

Whether it is the newest version of a popular computer game or the first-day sale of a new release, it has become normal to see hundreds of people lined up in all types of weather, sometimes even overnight, to be one of the first to make the purchase of a product before everyone else. To do so, many of these individuals will take time off from work, be away from their families, or call out sick just to get it before someone else.

The *New York Times*, on December 11, 2010, reported that "more than 400 Apple aficionados were waiting outside the company's New York flagship store on Fifth Avenue at 7 a.m., when the iPhone 3GS officially went on sale."[13] These lineups occur even though the same game or phone will be available the next day, the next week, or even the next month. At that point, there would be little or no lines, and there would even be a high probability that the same item will be available at a cheaper price.

---

[13] Jenna Wortham, "Opening Day: The iPhone 3GS," accessed April 22, 2013, *New York Times*. http://bits.blogs.nytimes.com/2009/06/19/opening-day-the-iphone-3g-s/?_r=0

Time away from work, used sick time, ignored responsibilities, adjusted priorities, and a reordered life all occur to accommodate and obtain the technology we depend on and have learned to love and now, for many, can't do without.

In one case, a mother reported to me that her fifteen-year-old son and his friend were involved in a gaming marathon over a recent weekend. She had to stop her son's play when it went late into early Sunday morning while her son's friend continued. On Monday morning, her son's friend passed out on his entry to school due to dehydration. He was admitted to the hospital requiring intravenous rehydration, attributed directly to his marathon gaming play over the weekend.

Just as in drug or alcohol addiction, in technology use, an individual's body typically requires a period of recovery after intense, extended use. This essentially creates an unhealthy cycle of intense use, followed by an emotional and/or physical crash as a means of recovering from the intense stimulation, dehydration, lack of physical movement, and possibly inadequate nutrition.

## Criterion #10: Being Less Socially, Occupationally, or Recreationally Involved

Have you ever been hospitalized with a serious illness, had a baby, or even moved to a new location? What do these three things have in common? Each results in changes of priorities. Having had a serious illness, I can tell you this means that health and life take on a new elevated meaning. The fast or comfort foods you may have loved before now may be seen as toxic, and inactivity is interpreted as a negative indicator of a potential slide toward some personal demise.

Having a baby changes the rules of a family and the way everyone relates. Everything changes! Gone is the sports car, and in its place is the family minivan. Money that used to go toward your hair or nails, beer, or car parts now goes toward baby formula and diapers. And for a while, the father is almost invisible while all of the attention is focused on the mother, that is, until the baby comes. Then both of the parents become almost invisible while all of the attention refocuses on the baby.

And if you suddenly need to move, all of your resources are marshaled to meet the deadlines of closings and settlements and then renovations and decorations. There is a refocusing from where you have been to where you're going to be.

As changes occur in life, you reprioritize to focus on those things you become involved with. Activities that demand your efforts and attention begin to overtake other activities, resulting in no longer having the time, resources, or attention to enjoy or find important things you used to enjoy.

Addiction is the exception to this rule. Addictions tend to override most previous priorities while they begin overriding your judgment. What would normally be important now pales in comparison to the compulsive nature of addiction. You are left with only one need, to feed your dependency. This can be a hard concept for many whose personalities are not as dependent to understand. But for those that are, rebalancing life toward the dependency can happen rapidly, impacting not only the person involved but everyone involved in his interpersonal system.

## Criterion #11: Continuied Use, Even When It Causes Problems

In my training sessions, I often ask the participants if anyone has ever found herself in any physically hazardous situations or putting someone else's safety at risk. I'll usually get several individuals admitting to a near-miss accident. They may find themselves providing inadequate supervision for a child or swerving to avoid a collision due to their phone, GPS, or other tech use. Yet when I continue my questioning, almost everyone who has created one of these situations continues to repeat the same hazardous behavior. Paraphrasing Albert Einstein, the definition of insanity is to repeat a behavior and expect a different result. I may be mistaken, but I think he was a rather smart man, yet none of these individuals I've just discussed would see herself as insane.

I firmly believe we have become so conditioned and so accepting of the use of technology in any situation, at any time of day, and in totally inappropriate instances that we just rationalize, justify, and accept this as normal.

Does anyone else see something wrong with standing in the exit doorway of a grocery store texting while a line of over a dozen angry shoppers stand with groceries in hand waiting for the person to finish texting or move? Or with the woman who walked off a pier, plunging into the river because she was texting and not looking where she was going? Maybe the man I overheard breaking up with his spouse over the phone while sitting on a public toilet? What made it worse was the fact that he then went on to blame her for being unreasonable for not understanding his need to view Internet pornography.

None of these occurances should be considered normal behavior and yet in the world we live in, conditioned by technology, shrugging these off is a normal occurance.

# 4

# This is Your Brain ...
# This is Your Brain on Technology

Do you remember the old Partnership for a Drug Free America TV commercials that said, "This is your brain ... this is your brain on drugs"? These commercials aired in the late 1980's, yet people still remember them. The commercials were also the topic of many jokes because so many people could relate to them.

The majority of people who have ever tried or used any kind of psychoactive substance know that drugs change the way you feel and think. They also know that not everyone who ever used a substance had their brain fried or experienced negative consequences. What they often fail to realize though is that, by making fun of the commercial, they are minimizing the damage that did occur in the thousands of deaths that occur annually due to drug use. We are now realizing (and research is showing) that technology, like abused substances, changes the way our brains work. For some individuals, the use of technology gets out of balance and becomes extremely detrimental, even fatal.

It is common for us to look to improve the way we feel. For some individuals, it is important to increase their connections and sense of belonging. For others, meditation, prayer, or exercise provides the respite needed to recharge. Work, hobbies, or engaging in face-to-face social interactions meets the needs of others. For many, a sense of security and safety allows them to go about their daily lives with less distraction from fears or anxiety. And for others, eating fills the void. Some use chemicals, compulsive behaviors, or an excessive use of technology to distance themselves from the discomfort of their daily life. There are numerous reasons why someone would want to retreat from daily life. The reasons are as varied as those who have them, from trying to escape the stress of daily life to a lack of fulfillment in the life they lead.

Often, retreating provides reflection or prayer or simply gives your brain a break. Taking time to just relax and think gives you a break from constant distractions and allows your nervous system to decompress. In the process you learn patience and gather insights into yourself and the world around you, and you may notice things that you have not noticed before. During periods of rest and meditation, I find I am energized and better able to attend to the needs of others and myself. Taking the time to empty my thoughts allows for new concepts, ideas, and perceptions to enter, many times in completely new and exciting ways.

But for some, alcohol, drugs, and now technology provide stimulation or sedation with perceptively no effort. Some recent studies have found that Facebook can create *flow states*, or periods where a person can actually experience a sense of disconnection from his or her immediate environment and lose track of time, after which he or she may experience exhilaration or fatigue.

Alternatives and shortcuts to concerted effort, focused attention, and sustained effort abound. Media promotions offer quick fixes and instant gratification, so why on earth would you want to spend years working to achieve something when you can buy it, steal it, or take shortcuts to the achievement process?

Young and older people alike need to learn to live life on life's terms. The use of computer games for short periods of an hour or two gives you the opportunity to distract yourself from life and take a mental break. But when you begin to withdraw from your family and long-term relationships, alter your life to accommodate gaming, and incur negative results, you have to look at improper technology use as a very real issue.

For most people, the overuse of technology is not a problem. But for others, it is extremely seductive, providing a constant flow of information, overstimulation, and an unending wealth of information and resources that often provide distraction and overstimulation for many individuals.

Many individuals, especially parents and teens, tell me they find a sense of safety and security in cell phone use, knowing they can reach anyone at any time they want to talk to him. For many though, the talking is almost exclusively via texting and email. If these are the primary forms of communication, how do we expect to have families, businesses, organizations, and schools where true interpersonal, face-to-face communication is valued and cherished?

For businesses, this overreliance on technology can be extremely disruptive, causing individuals to lose focus, and can result in negative consequences from a failure to meet deadlines to an injury when working around dangerous cargo or assembly lines. I've heard about more than one incident where an individual was injured on the job because of someone else's inattention.

In October 2008, a train crash in California killed 25 and injured another 135 commuters when an engineer was found to have been texting while piloting a train.[14] In November of that same year, a twenty-two-year-old woman was texting while driving and ran directly into the back of a stationary emergency vehicle, setting it on fire.[15] These instances may seem extreme; however, research indicates technology gadget usage is at an all-time high and steadily increasing.[16]

While I agree that there were often times indirect communication may have been preferred when speaking to my teens, these secondary forms of communication do not prepare us or them for how to interact, resolve conflict, or improve our interpersonal communications. We only get better through practice, and it can take a lifetime of practice to learn how to communicate well.

Social networks, Internet chat rooms, and texting all provide the sense of a highly controlled, anonymous environment. These interactions offer a level of disconnection and the perception of safety from intimate human contact with the perception of lacking all consequences. The Internet gives the illusion of legitimate

---

[14] "Train Engineer Was Texting Just Before California Crash," *Reuters*, October 2, 2008. http://www.reuters.com/article/2008/10/02/us-usa-train-crash-idUSN0152835520081002

[15] "Driving While Texting—Do You Know The Cost?" accessed April 22, 2013, CNN. http://www.cnn.com/2008/LIVING/wayoflife/11/14/aa.texting.while.driving/

[16] "Techy Tots: Britain Raising a Nation of Gadget Addicts," accessed April 22, 2013, *Easierlifestyle*. http://www.easier.com/82273-techy-tots-gadget-addicts.html

interpersonal interaction but lacks the full range of features of face-to-face interaction.

Because of the wide range of individuals you can interact with on the Internet, there is usually someone out there who will support and reinforce your ideas, regardless of the legitimacy or grounding in reality. The result can be misguided support from unknown individuals who are unbalanced or even downright unhealthy. For those with a poor self-image, social disabilities, depression, addictive tendencies, or lack of basic social skills, the potential validation of antisocial, immoral acts, and unhealthy behaviors is an ever-present problem. Unfortunately, there is always someone out there online to validate even the most deviant of behaviors. I believe this presents a significant threat to children and the child protection system. It also potentially elevates the risk of more aggressively antisocial behavior in our communities.

If someone generally acts inappropriately within a social group setting, someone in the group will signal some level of disapproval. I can recall being in middle school and acting in a way totally inconsistent with my traditional behavior. I was getting some attention for it so I kept it up. It wasn't until a couple of my friends came up to me on my walk home and told me it wasn't cool that I stopped and looked at my own behavior. Our peer groups in adolescents help us to normalize our behavior. Over time, the feedback we get teaches us what is acceptable and what is not. On the Internet, you can find some group out there that will approve even the most bizarre behaviors. For adolescents and susceptible adults, this can be dangerous, especially if they get into the wrong group.

Acceptance in a peer group is a high priority, not only for adolescents but also for adults. Just look at the number of members that Facebook and sites like LinkedIn have amassed. Being connected is incredibly important for many individuals, providing them a sense of belonging, continuity, and safety within a group.

For example, right after the 9/11 attacks, everyone I spoke to was buying cell phones for their family members and employees so they could get in touch with them in an emergency. Not only did these peer groups provide a social structure for many people, they also offered a sense of security. Even while experiencing phone line overloads and the inability to contact someone in a large-scale emergency, the illusion remains.

As the number of users increased, technology companies recognized they had an audience they could exert power to influence. This type of influence can be seen in other forms of technology as well, such as video games. A study at London's Hammersmith Hospital showed playing a war simulation video game stimulated neurotransmitters similar to those activated by addictive drugs during play.[17]

Additionally, those addicted to technology games demonstrate indicators of other addictions.[18] Many technology users feel an improved mood when using technology, want more when they stop, abandon attention to important tasks, and significantly underestimate, minimize, or deny their level of usage.

---

[17] C. J. Bench et al., "Evidence for Striatal Dopamine Release During a Video Game," *Letters to Nature* 393 (1998): 266–268. http://www.nature.com/nature/journal/v393/n6682/full/393266a0.html

[18] Norman Doidge, MD, *The Brain That Changes Itself* (New York: Penguin Books, 2007), 310. http://www.amazon.com/The-Brain-That-Changes-Itself/dp/0143113100

In his excellent book, *iBrain*, Dr. Gary Small clearly outlines the hazards associated with excessive exposure to technology.

The high-tech revolution also has contributed to many forms of anxiety, ranging from chronic generalized anxiety disorder to panic attacks that can be disabling. Baby boomers and seniors complain about computer anxiety and fear of the dangers of the Internet not only for themselves but also for their children and grandchildren. Parents with obsessive-compulsive disorders often find that when they are involved with digital technology, whether it's e-mail, shopping, or video gaming, they cannot control their impulses to continue him become addicted.[19]

Many adults today are presenting almost ADHD-like symptoms that could be attributed to their high level of technology use: increased anxiety, noticeable distractibility, inability to concentrate for extended periods of time, or lack in time management and/or organizational skills.

Have you ever been riding in the car humming a song or just listening to it when someone suddenly changes the channel? Or maybe you've been watching a TV show when the electricity suddenly goes out or someone changes the channel. Take a moment and think about what you were feeling at the time. More than likely, you may have felt annoyed or frustrated because you were listening to that song and wanted to hear it to the end. Our brains like closure and to have things finished. Once we have focused on a concept, process, or something of interest, our brains

---

[19] Small, Gary, M.D. *iBrain: Surviving the Technological Alteration of the Modern Mind* (New York: HarperCollins Publishers, 2008), 78. http://www.amazon.com/iBrain-Surviving-Technological-Alteration-Modern/dp/0061340340

like to finish processing the information (or thoughts) and to conclude the process before we move on.

In ideal situations, this is the thought cycle our brains go through:

- First, we see, hear, or feel something.
- Then we want to make sense of it and understand it so we can process the information.
- Finally, we form a conclusion or assumption or move on.

When we are unable to complete this thought cycle, we begin to feel anxious, unsettled, and incomplete. We begin to develop this sense of being unfinished when we can't complete the proper thought process. Without finishing a thought, our brain tends to want to complete the picture and may tend to even fill in the blanks where information is missing. When we do that, we make major assumptions.

A common scenario might look like the following: Music is in the background. You are working on two or three things. You are texting, email is coming in, and at the same time, you are on the phone. Your boss, child, spouse, or customer wants a question answered. Your brain becomes overwhelmed as you try to pay attention to everything. As you continue to pay attention to more and more things, you lose integrity in your brain's thought processes. It's like a computer opening more and more programs, which causes the computer to slow down at an ever-increasing rate until it finally shuts down. Our brains react very similarly, and stress develops as we try in vain to keep up.

So what do we do to compensate? As the amount of information increases, we try to get control of it by skimming information. We tend to gather information in volume but without depth or comprehensive understanding. A vast amount of basic data is obtained but without fully understanding the intricacies and nuances involved. As my friend and fellow speaker Tommy Hilken says, "It's like their learning is one inch deep and a mile wide!"[20]

---

[20] Tommy Hilken, personal interview, 2012.

# 5

# Always On

Tech addiction appears to be contributing to the anxiety impacting individuals today, ranging from mild or moderate anxiety to full-blown, disabling panic attacks.[21] Managers and parents consistently approach me after my presentations to voice concerns over a coworker's or child's constant and seemingly compulsive use of technology. With this in mind, whose brain chemistry predisposes them to be susceptible to technology addiction and dependence?

In *Breaking Free of the Web*, psychologist Kimberly Young found that those with reduced self-esteem and relationship deficits may be at an elevated risk to become addicted.[22] In her research, Linda Stone coined the phrase "continuous partial attention," observing the following about our society:

---

[21] Small, Gary, MD, 77. http://www.amazon.com/iBrain-Surviving-Technological-Alteration-Modern/dp/0061340340

[22] Kimberly Young, PsyD, *Breaking Free of the Web* (Cincinnati: St. Anthony Messenger Press, 2007), 38. http://www.amazon.com/Breaking-Free-Web-Catholics-Addiction/dp/B004LQ0JQ4

In a 24/7, always-on world, continuous partial attention used as our dominant attention mode contributes to a feeling of over-stimulation and to a sense of being unfulfilled. We are so accessible, we're inaccessible. The latest, greatest powerful technologies have contributed to our feeling increasingly powerless.[23]

We're so accessible that we're inaccessible.

As a note, Stone differentiates multitasking from continuous partial attention in that multitasking relies on automatic responses to familiar tasks, while continuous partial attention centers around staying constantly connected, giving minimal attention to numerous things as a result of the fear of becoming less significant by missing something.

Both of these states (multitasking and continuous partial attention) create their own problems. Multitasking can result in being distracted and missing details. When conditions change because we're not focusing or on autopilot, we can easily take things for granted.

With continuous partial attention, the potential for increased errors occurs when we learn basic information because we don't develop the tolerance and patience necessary to learn information with the depth and details needed to apply the information to real-life situations. In education and business, this could result in serious mistakes, injuries, and subsequent legal actions, such as when those going through school "fake it," resort to cheating, or find others to take shortcuts in the learning process.

---

[23] Linda Stone, "Continuous Partial Attention," accessed April 22, 2013. http://lindastone.net/qa/continuous-partial-attention/

The result is a stressed nervous system that constantly perceives itself to be in crisis. The body tends to react to high level of stimulation and involvement in technology as if it were in crisis. So what's the cost? Why is being highly stimulated over a period of time bad for us? This story might help illustrate the effects of a nervous system in crisis mode.

Years ago when our children were small, we had the opportunity to go to Colorado and stay at a small ranch set in the foothills of the Rocky Mountains outside of Pueblo. One afternoon, my wife had been sitting on the deck overlooking the meadow of multicolored wild flowers rimmed with bluish-green pine trees that extended well into the foothills that surrounded the cabin where we were staying. I came out to sit with her, and she began telling me how she had seen some wild turkeys feeding approximately 150 yards from the cabin and asked if we could go out and look for some wild turkey feathers to take home as souvenirs.

She pointed to a spot near the base of the trees at the bottom of a small rise covered with bushes. I didn't see any problem with her suggestion and thought it was a good idea so we got our then two-year-old daughter, Samantha, and set out through this vibrant field of wildflowers to the site where she had seen the turkeys. We jumped over a small stream and began looking on the ground for the feathers.

Suddenly, I noticed a small brown mound on the ground that resembled a loaf of pumpernickel bread from the bakery ... and it was steaming! I immediately had a sinking feeling in my stomach, and I turned to tell my wife that I thought we should get out of there.

Suddenly, there was a tremendously deep guttural roar that came from the rise just above us that sounded as if it emanated from a cavern at the center of the earth. I looked up and saw the bushes and small trees shaking. I immediately reached down, snatching Samantha under my arm like a football. Grabbing my wife by the hand, we took off running. A bear was chasing us!

As we ran, I can remember seeing only a small spot in front of me, which was the direction of the cabin. I could only hear the sound of bushes crashing behind us. This could have been my wife making that noise, but that is all I remember until we got closer to the cabin and looked back … only to find there was nothing coming behind us. Whew!

We ran up onto the deck and sat there panting with hearts pounding, unable to hear each other because of the stress having minimized our hearing. We didn't know whether we were going to pass out, throw up, or collapse. Our hearts continued to race for some time afterwards. We couldn't feel our hands or feet due to the chemicals released into our bodies as a result of this life-and-death situation.

Under extreme periods of stress, your hearing tends to diminish, focusing your attention solely on the potential threat at hand. Your eyesight narrows to focus on locating safety or avoiding potential threats. Circulation to your extremities decreases so you will bleed less if you are injured, allowing energy to be concentrated in the core of your body should it be necessary to flee or fight. Because of the intensity of the fear, it took us over an hour to begin to feel normal again, and I am sure we had stress hormones and various stress chemicals circulating in our bodies for hours afterwards.

Extended periods of hypervigilance and hyperawareness create increased stress, decreased focus, and impaired concentration. You can't stay in a constant state of high alert over any extended period of time without some negative impact. Under periods of high stress, naturally produced stimulating chemicals are released into the body and brain, circulating and allowing you to function with increased awareness.

Generally in the short run, they are beneficial, allowing you to respond more effectively and efficiently in the case of an emergency. However, when they are there over an extended period of time, they begin to have negative effects on the body. This can result in everything from an elevated heart rate, increased insulin output, and decreased blood flow to damage to the hippocampus, a portion of the brain responsible for learning and processing new information.

Research shows email interruptions increase stress while the information deluge creates distractions.[24] The ACE Study published in 1998 by Kaiser Permanente and the Centers for Disease Control and Prevention found that diabetes, heart disease, substance abuse, and suicide were higher than the national norm for adults raised in homes as children where crisis was a constant.[25] These findings highlight the potential for increased medical costs, sick time, and family time being taken to deal with illness or injury caused by the abuse or overuse of technology.

---

[24] Matt Richtel, "Multitasking Hurts Brain's Ability to Focus, Scientists Say," *Seattle Times*, June 6, 2010. http://seattletimes.com/html/nationworld/2012049123_webmultitask07.html

[25] Centers for Disease Control and Prevention, *The Adverse Childhood Experiences Study*, accessed April 22, 2013. http://www.cdc.gov/ace/

One area of technology where people are increasingly dependent—and yet often don't take time to think about its effects—is television. TV shows have increased their rate of change in scenes and actions in response to our need for more stimulation and immediate gratification. If you would like to get a sense of this, spend an evening watching old TV shows or, better yet, go to the library and take out some old TV shows on DVD. Watch those shows for approximately fifteen minutes, and then watch an equal amount of time of Saturday morning cartoons. You'll notice that the pace of the old TV shows was much slower than programming of today. The storyline and scenes from the Saturday morning cartoons change at an incredible rate, exceeding the pace experienced in real life.

Few people stop to question how these increasing rates impact our brains. However, this increase could contribute to a lack of patience and understanding amongst coworkers or students. Many managers I speak with today tell me that interpersonal problems are taking up more of their time today than they did ten years ago. And while we can't attribute this solely to technology, I think we need to look at it.

Video games are another area of technology impacting our brains. After studying the habits of gamers, game developers have modified the incentive systems within their games to correspond directly to the players' desire to be rewarded, enticing players to press on. Oftentimes, developers know exactly how many times a person will try without giving up. As the game goes on, the rewards come more frequently or in stages to keep the player engaged longer. The longer a person is engaged, the more invested she becomes and the more she identifies with the game. In 2010 alone, gamers in general spent approximately thirteen hours per week gaming.[26]

Most of these games involve high levels of stimulating game play, including global interaction with other players through the Internet. When you play video games into the evening hours, your brain can become overstimulated, making it extremely difficult to calm down and fall asleep. And these chemicals don't go away right away.

Like my previous story of the bear chasing me, it takes time for our bodies to calm down from playing these stimulating games. The result? Even if you are able to fall asleep, you may wake up within a couple hours due to the circulating chemicals in our bodies. You are tired enough to get to sleep, but after a short period of rest, you reawaken. You have not had enough sleep to have a full night's rest, but you can't sleep due to the stimulating effects of the game. Often, sleep eludes gamers, and they lay there awake, unable to relax.

A physician told me of a parent who came in with her son for treatment for what she described as a sleep disorder. He asked about the son's evening habits of eating, drinking, and recreation. After speaking with the son, he asked the parent to discontinue allowing the son to have caffeine in the evening and to limit his use of video games in the evening. Guess what? No more sleep disorder!

In another instance, a parent related that her son was having problems getting up in the morning and staying attentive in

---

[26] "Extreme Gamers Spend Two Full Days Per Week Playing Video Games," accessed April 22, 2013, *NPD Group: Behind Every Business Decision*. https://www.npd.com/wps/portal/npd/us/news/press-releases/pr_100527b/

school all day. At my suggestion, she stopped his video gaming in the evening, and she reported vast improvement in his sleep habits and staying attentive in school, and he was a much more pleasant person.

It is also common for gamers and many high school students for that matter to use caffeine or energy drinks to maintain their energy levels during a gaming marathon or in the morning before and during school. Just before Circuit City closed, I was looking for bargains when my son-in-law came over from the gaming section with a small box containing a "Stay Up All Night Kit." It contained a can of energy drink, some stimulant gum, an eighty-hour energy spray, and beef jerky, everything one might need to stay wired.

According to Johns Hopkins University Medical Center, caffeine in energy drinks, gums, and sprays, like in this kit, can cause everything from mild nervousness to panic disorders. The daily average in the United States is approximately 280 milligrams of caffeine. At 100 milligrams, you are on the brink of caffeine dependence and may experience withdrawal symptoms.[27] Many of the energy drinks hover just under 100 milligrams.[28]

This may be a relief for some parents until they realize that many young people drink several of these, one after another, to get the desired effect. It is common to see high school students walking into school with one energy drink in their hands and

---

[27] Johns Hopkins Bayview Medical Center, "Information about Caffeine Dependence," accessed April 22, 2013. http://www.caffeinedependence.org/caffeine_dependence.html

[28] Center for Science in the Public Interest, "Caffeine Content of Food & Drugs," accessed April 22, 2013. http://www.cspinet.org/new/cafchart.htm

another one or two in their pockets or book bag. How many adolescents or adults use these substances at the recommended dosages and in moderation? For many, if a little is good, a lot is better!

In a class of social workers I was teaching on adolescent trends, a gentleman in his early thirties came up to me. He had been working in a prison setting but recently had to leave that job to take on a less demanding position. He then went on to tell me that he enjoyed working out, evident by his obvious physical development, and he had been told by his doctors that he had experienced three to four ministrokes, which they attributed directly to his intake of energy drinks and energy bars. Here was this well-intentioned man trying to be a better role model in the prison system, now concerned about his health because of the chemicals he had been ingesting.

Many parents buy these products for their children, not realizing they often contain ingredients that are diuretics and stimulants. When they are consumed to hydrate before sporting events, they may actually contribute to dehydration. Our brains need oxygen and water in order to function. Without adequate fluid intake, not only do we impact physical performance, we affect brain functions as well.[29]

It is also common for individuals to sit at a computer for extended periods without taking breaks, especially if they are in the midst of an all-night gaming session. This can not only result in a reduction of oxygen and blood flow to the brain but

---

[29] M. J. McKinley and A. K. Johnson, "The Physiological Regulation of Thirst and Fluid Intake," *News in Physiological Sciences* 19 (2004): 1–6. http:// physiologyonline.physiology.org/content/19/1/1.long

can also contribute to eye strain, posture issues, and stress-related ailments.[30] Some individuals have even been sedentary for such a long period of time that they actually developed blood clots and died.

Current research shows that violent video games and movies may also be changing our brains and subsequently our behavior. Admittedly, playing video games may actually prepare the user with skills necessary to replicate the behavior when an opportunity arises. If you are a pilot or surgeon, that could be great news. Dexterity could be improved. Reaction times are reduced in preparation for unanticipated complications or conditions played out in a cyber world where no one gets hurt or dies from a mistake. Research shows "mentally rehearsing a situation helps us perform better when we encounter that situation in the physical environment. Similarly, hearing stories acts as a kind of mental flight simulator, preparing us to respond more quickly and effectively."[31]

However, if you are a young person with an immature brain who cannot yet make fully informed adult decisions, this could be hazardous without developed coping skills. In the *New York Times* article, "From Students, Less Kindness for Strangers?" researchers attribute a 30 percent decrease in empathy over the past thirty years to "video games, social media, reality TV, and

---

[30] Healthy Healthy List, "Top 4 Health Problems Caused by Computer Use," accessed April 22, 2013. http://heheli.com/business/top-4-health-problems-caused-by-computer-use/

[31] Chip Heath and Dan Heath, *Made To Stick: Why Some Ideas Stick and Others Die* (New York: The Random House Publishing Group, 2007), 18. http://www.amazon.com/Made-Stick-Ideas-Survive-Others/dp/1400064287

hyper-competition."[32] Decreased empathy relates to criminality, violence, and numerous other antisocial behaviors.

While this manual is not a condemnation of technology, I want it to make you think and raise important questions about its use. These are important questions because the answers impact our lives and the lives of those we care about.

Current research shows the brain goes through a tremendous amount of development prior to birth and in the first few months of life and continues in its advancement, maturing well into our late twenties and early thirties. The brain reflects the environment in which it forms, positively impacted by enriched environments or delayed and diminished by hostility, overstimulation, and stress.

In *The Mind and the Brain*, Jeffrey M. Schwartz, MD, states that sensory experiences change the brain relative to the experiences they encounter.[33] Within the first twelve months of life, connections in the brain begin to grow stronger if they are stimulated and reinforced, but they are pruned away if they are not reinforced and utilized. Pruning occurs at various stages in development, continuing through puberty and potentially beyond.

Physical workouts help to make our bodies stronger because the targeted exercises we use—and the specific actions we intentionally practice—make certain muscles stronger. We have to make sure the exercises we do strengthen those muscles we

---

[32] Pamela Paul, "From Students, Less Kindness for Strangers?" *New York Times*, June 25, 2010. http://www.nytimes.com/2010/06/27/fashion/27StudiedEmpathy.html

[33] Jeffrey M. Schwartz, MD, *The Mind and the Brain: Neuroplasticity and the Power of Mental Force* (New York: ReganBooks, HarperCollins, 2002). http://www.amazon.com/The-Mind-Brain-Neuroplasticity-Mental/dp/0060988479

want to enhance. Targeting only some muscles and neglecting others would make us unbalanced and could actually cause more harm than good. Besides, we would look extremely weird!

In similar fashion, we need to make sure the habits we get into via our technology use are those we want to reinforce and perpetuate as we maintain balance with the rest of our lives. It is important to note that "developing teens have the power to determine their own brain development, to determine which connections survive and which don't, whether they do art, or music, or sports, or video games."[34] This may help explain why many adolescents who extensively play video games, text, use Facebook, and surf the Internet are scattered in their thinking. Their attention to so many different things has the tendency to defocus their attention, inhibiting their concentration and ability to focus on any one thing. Yet in high schools and college environments, most course work and a huge portion of their social interaction involves technological communication.

On the positive side, individuals learn to digest massive amounts of information very rapidly. They learn extremely rapid mental processing and hand-eye coordination via data manipulation, simulations, and video games. Their ability to develop social networks grows exponentially as they email, text, and tweet. From these things, it would appear that an individual's ability to multitask becomes highly developed within a social networking framework.

The negative side, though, is that those things you pay attention to tend to build stronger connections, resulting in

---

[34] Ibid., 129. http://www.amazon.com/The-Mind-Brain-Neuroplasticity-Mental/dp/0060988479

more substantial brain structures in specific areas. You are best at the things you practice. Whether or not we are practicing in ways beneficial to the brain is another story. The activities you engage in act as practice sessions that either develop skills and abilities to support brain structure development, aiding the brain's highly technical abilities or habits that impede the development of those areas of the brain supporting social and interpersonal skills.

Due to the lack of stimulation and utilization in areas of the brain necessary to maximize an individual's capabilities for social interactions, many such individuals today present with almost autistic-type behaviors. They often avoid eye contact, obsess over electronic stimulation, have poor interpersonal skills, avoid development of intimacy, and so forth. Many individuals report finding it faster, easier, and less work to form online relationships, abandoning the quest for interpersonal relationships traditionally established over extended periods of time.

In my discussions with parents and educators, a constant concern expressed is the amount of time that young people are spending in electronic communication instead of face-to-face personal interactions. Many researchers support my concern that we may be creating a generation who may mimic Asperger's symptoms: a lack of boundary awareness, reduced social skills, decreased interpersonal communication skills, and social isolation.

BBC News reported on September 15, 2009, that research conducted by the Cranfield School of Management, Northampton Business School, and AJM Associates revealed that technology negatively impacted student concentration and spelling while also impairing the ability to learn.[35] Here are some of the findings for the 267 students surveyed between the ages of eleven and eighteen:

- 63 percent felt addicted to the Internet.
- 53 percent felt addicted to their mobile phones.
- 53 percent spent at least thirty minutes a day on their mobile phones.
- 30 percent spent at least one to two hours per day surfing the Internet.
- 26 percent spent six or more hours a day on the Internet.
- 17 percent indicated they spend more than three hours a day on their phones.

In a Reuters news report from April 24, 2010, a University of Maryland study "asked 200 students to give up all media for one full day and found that after 24 hours many showed signs of withdrawal, craving, and anxiety, along with an inability to function well without their media and social links."[36]

With these symptoms of withdrawal present, is it no wonder that research is showing similarities in the way the brain is stimulated by drugs, sex, music, and, yes, technology use?

[35] "Tech addiction 'harms learning,'" *BBC News*, September 15, 2009. http://news.bbc.co.uk/2/hi/uk_news/education/8256490.stm

[36] Walden Siew, "U.S. Students Suffering from Internet Addiction—study," accessed April 22, 2013, *Reuters*. http://www.reuters.com/article/2010/04/23/us-internet-addicts-life-idUSTRE63M4QN20100423

# 6

# Sex, Drugs, and Rock and Roll

The combination of sexual content and technological innovation is further compounding the problematic impact of technology misuse. Today, cybersex has gone mainstream. "In his 2001 *New York Times Magazine* story "Naked Capitalists," Frank Rich asserts, 'The $4 billion that Americans spend on video pornography is larger than the annual revenue accrued by either the N.F.L., the N.B.A. or Major League Baseball.'"[37] Imagine what that figure is today!

Here are some alarming statistics released by Family Safe Media in 2006 regarding the extent of pornography consumption in the United States:[38]

- $3,075.64 is spent every second on pornography.
- Every second, 28,258 Internet users are viewing pornography.

---

[37] "How Porn Went from Boom to Bust," accessed April 22, 2013, *Forbes.* http://www.forbes.com/sites/susannahbreslin/2012/07/11/how-porn-went-from-boom-to-bust/

[38] Family Safe Media, "Pornography Statistics," accessed April 22, 2013. http://www.familysafemedia.com/pornography_statistics.html

- Every second, 372 Internet users are typing adult terms into search engines.
- Every thirty-nine minutes, a new pornographic video is being created in America.

And how much of this is happening at work? From one report, 25 percent of workers view porn sites during work hours.[39]

The computer has provided the sex industry with immediate and easy access to almost every home, dorm room, office, cell phone, and Wi-Fi location. Previously you would have to leave your home and drive or walk to a local store that specialized in—or in some way provided—adult reading material. Today, even if you're not looking for it, pornography can still find its way onto your computer or mobile device.

Historically places where you could access pornography were set apart from mainstream shopping areas because there was a social taboo about being seen going into one of these establishments. Today, adult-themed movies are available free of charge on the Internet, are accessible in your hotel room at some of the best hotels in the world, and delivered on demand to your living room, bedroom, dorm room, or office. On the Internet, sex is delivered through a myriad of options including pictures, videos, online chat rooms, arranged meetings, and even through cybersex via avatars. By the time this guide is published, there will likely be other methods of dispensing sexual pleasures that can't even be imagined.

---

[39] Anna Kuchment, "The Tangled Web of Porn in the Office," *Newsweek*, November 28, 2008. http://archive.is/xWFEp

Many young people—and, yes, even adults—have developed a new method of flirting called "sexting." This recent phenomenon involves the distribution of suggestive, sexually inviting, and sometimes semi-nude or nude photos over your phone or email. Often, incomplete images are sent of various body parts in the hope of getting or enticing a response. If these pictures are of an underage person, even if someone underage sends it, the individual could open himself up to being charged as a distributor of child pornography. When images like these are sent utilizing a business-owned phone or computer, legal charges and job dismissal could result. If these images are "sexted" to a subordinate, sexual harassment charges could be levied, and companies could be held liable for the employee's harassment.

"Sexting" is a serious issue because many people do not recognize that, once a text or email message has been sent, it can essentially circulate the Internet forever. This fact could easily lead to embarrassing situations in which someone's semi-nude or nude photos come back to haunt him. In one case, a Huston police officer with a twenty-year history on the force was suspended from the police department for pictures taken in her private life.[40] In another incident, a guidance counselor was fired from her job because of racy pictures taken almost twenty years earlier.[41]

---

[40] Victoria Cavaliers, "Houston Police Sergeant Faces Dismissal over Posting Nude Photos of Herself Online," *New York Daily News*, October 3, 2012. http://www.nydailynews.com/news/national/mom-faces-firing-online-nude-pix-article-1.1173604

[41] "High School Guidance Counselor Fired Over Racy Lingerie Photos That She Posted 17 Years Ago," accessed April 22, 2013, *MailOnline*. http://www.dailymail.co.uk/news/article-2214109/Tiffany-Webb-High-school-guidance-counselor-fired-racy-lingerie-photos.html

"Revenge porn" has become a new method of harming those you have had relationships with. Individuals are taking home movies that were taken in the midst of their relationship, and once the relationship goes south, they may want to get back at the other person for being wronged. There are numerous sites where you can post adult videos of your former significant partner for the entire world to see. And when individuals have contacted these companies to get these damaging videos removed, they were rebuffed and unsuccessful in their attempts. Currently, a number of sites are reporting legal action has been taken to limit these types of humiliating displays, but the ease of removal is in question.

The things you do online have can have a multitude of consequences, such as jeopardizing your dream job. Many human resource managers tell me they regularly and consistently check Facebook, LinkedIn, Tumblr, and other social networking sites to see if the person interviewing for a position is forthright and consistent with what they see on those pages. It has become common hiring practice for employers to include an Internet search of the applicant's name.

Some individuals may not recognize that this electronic trail will follow them as they go through their life, either enhancing their potential reputation or becoming an embarrassing shadow silently following them for years, if not the rest of their lives!

When you interact with individuals on the Internet, you're not experiencing face-to-face interactions necessary for developing or honing the skills to become more effective and accurate in social situations. Having social decorum and conversation skills, developing and progressing through relationships, testing limits, developing tolerance, handling frustration, and learning to delay gratification are all skills necessary for a life of long-term relationships with other people.

When you only have to interact with someone intermittently and from a distance, it's far easier to be tolerant and forgiving. However, in the real world, it's often necessary to work with people you don't agree with or don't like or are just disagreeable. Yet, it is important to see different points of view and work through them while learning to respect, appreciate, and even tolerate other people.

Those individuals with the ability to read social context and develop an effective repertoire of interpersonal skills do far better in business, relationships, and life. Electronic communications often fail to provide the context and nuances necessary for people to adequately communicate.

With so much of the Internet being a platform for presenting and marketing, it is no wonder that those growing up with no memory of a life before computers often find it difficult to effectively problem-solve and work in groups. Resolving real-life problems often takes time and perseverance, and an answer is not simply a mouse click away. This desire for instant gratification with minimal repercussions makes cyber relationships and virtual affairs all the more enticing. Unrealistic expectations are also reinforced online via the repetitive viewing of airbrushed, light-enhanced actors and actresses who perform with unconditional acceptance and without consideration for feelings, respect, personal needs, or consequences.

Sexual intimacy is often then replaced with the quest for the proper techniques to achieve maximum physical satisfaction.

This minimizes the value of the interpersonal relationship and objectifies the partner.

When individuals who are primarily socializing through the Internet run into problems, they often turn to the Internet for solutions. Here again, if you have access to a large enough pool of individuals, you will find someone somewhere who will validate even the most dysfunctional, disturbed, or destructive thoughts and behaviors.

It's not the technology that's the problem; rather, it's the way it's being used. The problem for many individuals today is that it takes effort and hard work in order to wade through all of the information on the Internet. This provides a threat to those who are inexperienced and naïve or those with cognitive disorders, social inadequacies, addiction, and impulse problems because stumbling onto deceptive or downright pornographic sites can be so accidental, especially with the promise of opportunity, success, and immediate resolution of everyday problems only a click away.

With the proliferation of sex and sexual content on the Internet, there is a tendency to develop a false sense of intimacy, especially sexual in nature, with others in cyberspace. The Internet provides the perception of anonymity, increasing the tendency for experimentation otherwise restrained by personal fear or socially imposed values. The perception is that, once you close your office or bedroom door, what you do is private.

Often, virtual interactions, whether in online chat rooms or via Internet role-play, are perceived as harmless because they are nonphysical interactions. When encouraged by the perception of invisibility, there is a tendency for individuals to stray into areas that might otherwise be taboo. Because these interactions are virtual, they are often viewed as innocent and are rationalized away simply as a form of experimentation rather than a form of relational cheating.

Catfishing (or Cat Fishing) describes interactions with individuals online to create and maintain relationships for the purpose of manipulating or taking advantage of another individual. These relationships have made national headlines, and in many, not so public cases, they have proven very costly to reputations and mental health. In some cases, they have cost lives.

This sense of anonymity prompts individuals into acting on whatever thoughts cross their minds, which would normally be restrained out of guilt or fear of being caught. For young people who are working through their own sexual identity issues, this type of experimentation can allow for greater latitude than would normally be attempted in real life. For the developing adolescent, this can create a tremendous amount of confusion, especially when ill-advised advice is dispensed online.

Parents need to be aware of the influences available on the Internet through social networking sites, chat rooms, or websites promoting every type of view possible. It is also common for sexual and social predators to pose as children online. Adult content is everywhere online nowadays, and it is extremely important for parents to be checking Internet histories and discussing the dangers of practicing or delving into values different than those promoted by the family.

Virtual platforms utilizing avatars have been used to even further proliferate adult content on the Internet. In the platform Second Life, you are able to go in and create a virtual person (an avatar) to represent yourself. Many individuals were introduced to these virtual people in the movie *Avatar*.[42] An avatar is a virtual representation of the person creating it. When you go into a virtual platform like Second Life, you are asked to provide written information about yourself, and then you are directed to a space where you can create an avatar. In some of these platforms, the only requirement to move from the children's portion into the adult portion is to click the button indicating you're an adult.

The information provided does not necessarily have to be legitimate; nor does the avatar have to resemble anything that has to do with reality. Often, individuals spend a tremendous amount of time crafting their avatars so they can present themselves in an idealized state. The amount of time put into creating the avatar causes the individual to become highly invested in this alternative personality. Because reality does not limit you, your avatar can be created in any anatomical form you would like, allowing you to augment those areas of your body that you want enhanced while minimizing others. This can realistically become an idealized image of oneself, emboldening a sense of self-confidence in the avatar that the person in real life may not experience.

The emotional health of the individual will depend on how well he or she is able to maintain the balance between the virtual and real world. Most people can go on to exchange information, ideas, and experiences with other people and come out of the game relatively unaffected. However, there are those people who have difficulty separating reality from fiction. Young children, adolescents, and adults with cognitive deficits are especially susceptible because of the immature development

---

[42] James Cameron, Director, *Avatar*, 2009. http://www.avatarmovie.com/index.html

of the brain, their need to experiment with life in general, or the inability to adequately process and understand the consequences of their actions.

In real life, we get feedback from the real world as to what does and doesn't work and/or what is and isn't acceptable, tolerated, or beneficial. In the virtual world, however, we do not as readily receive these social cues.

In many of the avatar-manipulated games, you can meet people, get into relationships, get married, consummate the relationship, and then go on to have children. Some sites will allow you to go on to interact with virtual people, while others will allow you to build an avatar of your choice for a totally virtual relationship.

When you continually view and engage in these types of interactions and experiences, you begin neurologically participating and identifying with the onscreen people. This can be both positive and negative. Many of these platforms allow you to experience activities you would never have the opportunity to do otherwise.

For someone who can't get to various locations, websites and virtual platforms offer wonderful images and possibilities through the opportunity to wander with your avatar as you visit a foreign land, browse through a museum, visit a college campus, or meet with individuals from around the world in a centralized virtual location. Because your avatar is in a virtual world, it can go underwater, fly, view things from a 360-degree perspective, and try things that normally would be impossible for us to do.

But virtual platforms aren't without their downsides, especially when it comes to adult-themed and violent content. By merely going onto a search engine and typing "virtual reality games," you come up with an almost unlimited supply of options. I came up with 7.72 million results when I used Google to search for "virtual reality games."

Picking one at random, I entered the site and typed in bogus information indicating I was twenty years old, and I was immediately taken to a main webpage providing a variety of options for me to purchase access to X-rated content and interactions. Any child could have done the same exact thing and obtained access to sexual content. As mentioned in chapter 3, a priest friend of mine told me of two annulments he had to preside over that were directly related to online gaming and an affair an individual was carrying on within the context of the game.

Today with a few clicks of the mouse, you can have access to and practice just about any type of experience, perversion, and immoral activity that can be conceived. As of now, none of this is illegal because it is all virtual. Whether it is practicing pedophilia or forcing someone into a sex act with your avatar, it's all technically legal because no physical act takes place, and in the eyes of the law, no one is harmed.

The problem here is that, by practicing a behavior repeatedly, you begin to build a structure in your brain to accommodate the behavior. Just like playing the piano allows you to improve, engaging in any act over time, even if that act is virtual, prepares you to carry out the behavior in real life. This should be scary for any parent, educator, clergy, health-care provider, or concerned community member.

# 7

# Networking Nirvana

As the preceding chapter shows, a false sense of intimacy can be quickly created via the Internet. So powerful is this perceived connection that individuals may find themselves engaging in activities and/or relationships they would not otherwise be involved with. This is troublesome because true intimacy takes time to develop.

Honest, meaningful, and intimate relationships occur when people invest in their relationships. I've identified four Ts that are present in developing intimate long-term relationships:

- You need **time** to exchange ideas, to see if you are in agreement with that other person, and to really see if she is consistent in what she says and does. Time tells the truth in interactions when you find that the person you are in the relationship with is honest and consistent.
- **Trust** is tested over time as to whether the other person is trustworthy. You share information and wait to see what the other person does with it. You see if her actions are consistent with her words and if you can rely on her. Trusting someone comes only when she proves to be

trustworthy. Anyone can carry off a façade of caring for a while, but no one can consistently maintain this over extended periods of time. Trust is built by identifying boundaries for healthy interaction and demonstrating respect for each other's boundaries.

- **Tenacity** is demonstrated by working through problems and misunderstandings and developing the relationship over time through the recognition of benchmarks of experience.
- **Triumph** is celebration of the time invested in building the relationship, the value of developing trust, and the recognition and valuing your tenacity as you work through problems.

Together, the four Ts form the foundation for building respectful, responsible relationships with integrity.

Often when relationships develop quickly (for example, via the Internet), they are often established without the test of time to determine the legitimacy of the claim of being trustworthy. If we become used to getting immediate gratification, then tenacity to stay at it when times are tough may not be something we have the tolerance for or recognize as valuable. In social and electronic media, the rapid exchange of information results in the perception and illusion of intimacy without the test of time to prove its authenticity.

Information is easy to relate to over the Internet due to the perceived isolation created by the computer screen. In the perceived safety of your room, office, dorm, or kitchen, there is a sense that you are alone and no one is watching what you do or say or to whom you say it to. I doubt the Rutgers University student who secretly videotaped his roommate in a relationship with another male student ever dreamed that the video he created would cause the extent of damage and loss of life that it did.

In chat rooms, Facebook, and email relationships, information is often shared with a tremendous amount of fearless transparency. This puts the person relating to the information in a vulnerable position because there is no way to verify the identity of the person on the other side of the screen. Online, you can create any persona that you choose to construct. Utilizing this persona over time allows a person to embellish and re-image it, that is, trying it on to see how it fits. Over time, the individual may actually begin to take on aspects of this persona as she redefines herself for others.

And when is all this information shared? With everyone being accessible twenty-four hours a day via cell phones or email, boundaries seem to be eroding between business and personal time. Personally, I know at times I have found myself ignoring my own rules for containing my technology dependence.

One Saturday several years ago, my cell phone rang when I was out fishing with my daughter. Looking at it, I knew right away that it was a new client of mine. Here I was, having time with my daughter fishing that I could never replace, and I still took the call. This was a time for my daughter and I, and I mismanaged it by allowing work to bleed into my personal life and time with my family.

My daughter is now grown and married and doing well. However, I cherish every minute that I get to see her, and now that she lives on the opposite end of the country, every minute I get is even more precious. It is only in retrospect that I regret that I took any time away. You only have a limited time with your children and your family members and living the life you are in. The time we have with our families is vital for maintaining personal relationships with those we care for.

Here are some alarming statistics about how we allow technology to blur the lines between our work and our personal lives:[43]

- Over 86 percent of employees use office email for personal reasons.
- 65 percent of Internet usage in the workplace is not work related.
- 64 percent of employees have received politically incorrect or offensive emails at work.
- 20 percent of employees surf the Internet at least ten times a day.
- 67 percent of employers are using the information technology (IT) staff to monitor one or more forms of employee electronic communication.

Years ago, no one would have thought of sitting and writing personal letters during a work day, but today, emailing during work seems like a normal activity for many.

There are numerous times that I can recall entering a store or other business and finding it hard to even get someone's attention due to his or her texting or emailing. Checking into a

---

[43] Carolyn G. Burnette, "Employee Abuse of Technology the Ever-Changing Workplace Challenge." http://www.shawvalenza.com/pubs/Employee%20 Abuse%20of%20Technology.pdf

hotel recently, I approached the front desk and noticed that the young lady behind the desk was texting. I waited a moment for her to finally notice me, at which point, she said, "I'll be with you in just a moment." She went on to complete her text and then set the phone down and asked, "Can I help you?" I had two thoughts:

- My first thought was regarding the theft of service from her employer. She might not be doing work of the establishment while she was texting.
- My second thought was that she was certainly not focused on the customer because she had me wait while she completed her message.

Has the use of social media really become so pervasive and important that it is a justified personal activity, even at work? These behaviors would not be tolerated on an assembly line or in the shipping department, yet in numerous worksites, they are common practice. I believe we are seeing the erosion of relationship integrity in our businesses and personal lives. Neither are we being served well due to the constant distractions of diffused boundaries and the overuse and abuse of technology.

Business and personal relationships benefit from firm boundaries and expectations. In the workplace today, there is confusion over what role people are playing at that particular moment. At what point are they working for the business or attending to personal matters?

Is it fair to your employer if you sit at work and continually type text messages to family members? And are you really giving your clients the service and attention they deserve when you're standing on the side of a soccer match stealing time away from your children and family? I'm constantly hearing stories of family members visiting for special events, only to have some members of the contingent spending most of their time texting others who are not in attendance.

This problem is compounded by the fact that so much of our work today relies on social networking, texting, and email. It would be nice to think that you could go through your day only checking your email once or twice every few hours. Many individuals, however, rely on email and texting as a primary form of communication, even though this is mostly an inexact form of communication. The interesting thing about this constant checking of email is that it tends to interrupt the work being done and may actually be more disruptive than we had realized because only around "40 percent of the time you go back to what you were doing."[44] Many people actually answer their email every time it "dings," signaling a new mail message has arrived. This constant disruption begins to ramp up your nervous system and interrupts your thought processes to the point that it may be difficult to return your attention to your work.

To counteract this, some individuals may begin to post Post-It notes around their computer screen to remind them of where they were or what they were involved in. Not only is this often unsuccessful, it clutters up your visual field, causing even more chaos for you internally. We tend to pay limited attention to multiple things and then wonder why we have difficulty focusing.

---

[44] "'Interruption Science': Costly Distractions at Work," *NPR*, October 14, 2005. http://www.npr.org/templates/story/story.php?storyId=4958831

Focus is essential in order to be productive. Here are six tips for getting past "Networking Nirvana" and regaining focus in your work and your personal life:

- Set a timer for when you will check your email next.
- Install software on your computer that allows you to only access the Internet or email a certain number of minutes per day.
- Check your email two to four times per day.
- Place cell phones and other distractions in your desk drawer when they are not being used so you are not tempted to use them when working.
- Discuss with office coworkers how you can be supportive of each other as you seek to adhere to personal policies around technology use.
- Limit yourself to email and only one or two different forms of social networking sites.

When a message comes in, consider if you really need to interrupt what you are doing, or can it wait?

Marshall Goldsmith, in *Mojo: How to Get it, How to Keep it, How to Get it Back if you Lose it*, suggests we ask ourselves two questions to evaluate our use of the Internet:[45]

- How much long-term benefit or meaning did I experience in this activity?

---

[45] Marshall Goldsmith, *Mojo: How to Get It, How to Keep It, How to Get It Back If You Lose It* (New York: Hyperion Books, 2009), 36. http://www.amazon.com/Mojo-How-Keep-Back-Lose/dp/B003XU7VME

- How much short-term satisfaction or happiness did I experience in this activity?

Goldsmith believes that just asking these questions will do two things:

- It will cause you to evaluate the level of meaning you experience while on the computer.
- The mere fact that you evaluated the session will make you think beforehand about what you are doing.

This may actually help limit endless hours of mindless surfing in Networking Nirvana.

# 8

# Technology's Impact on Education

Businesses need to be very aware of the impact Networking Nirvana can have on their employees. But businesses are not the only institutions being impacted by increased dependence on technology. The use of technology in schools has also grown exponentially each year with increased utilization of whiteboards, closed-circuit or school/community-based TV stations, assignments being posted online, and parent-teacher interactions over the Internet. These uses of technology allow for immediate and far greater dissemination of information than could ever be achieved without it.

Students as well as teachers are learning to research, manipulate data, prepare presentations, and interact with greater frequency, thanks to electronic communication. The percentage of colleges and high schools requiring students to submit papers and reports electronically grows daily, requiring less and less need to interact personally with fellow students or staff.

Some schools issue laptops or tablet computers for students and/or faculty to do classwork, study, collaborate online, and email. Classes are, at times, presented virtually through nontraditional education systems and online schools.

Administrators and teachers tell me that most teachers are rewarded for their use of technology, encouraging them to use it as much as possible. Those who are the most innovative and successful in their use of technology get rewarded with incentives from their district and various levels of government. In some cases, there is almost no need to attend class, interact with others face-to-face, or deal with people directly at all. The advantage of this is better access to information, and for those who don't want to, they don't have to interact with people unless it is absolutely necessary.

In addition, some schools have gone completely paperless, allowing for assignments, group projects, and tests all to be completed and submitted electronically with barely any personal interaction. Teachers are incorporating texting and email into their lessons. In one instance, children were encouraged to text their parents during class for information for a report. (I wonder if parents are working during these class times.) Colleges incorporate group discussion into their curriculum through web-based platforms, which allow multiple individuals to provide input, record sessions, and compare notes online.

Creativity, communication, interaction, and information sharing have all been enhanced in the classroom through every conceivable form of technology. The problem lies in that, with every advantage that comes along, there are also disadvantages. With decreased interpersonal interaction comes reduced person-to-person skills and capacity to read social and facial cues. These skills are necessary for effective communication between individuals in face-to-face interactions, and they are essential in the development of interpersonal relationships.

Schools need to properly cultivate the next generation's workforce, public servants, parents, and partners. Yet many schools report their inability to curtail cell phone use in school. Students report rampant cheating via cell phones in high school and college, while many districts seem to be at a loss on how to manage tech abuse in the school. Teachers tell me that students constantly get calls—some from parents—in class. Boundaries of appropriate use seem to be dissolving. What will this mean as students move from the school to the work setting?

The owner of a small pizza shop reported that he has a high level of turnover. The high school students he hires don't seem to be able to work without constantly being distracted by their cell phones or using them when they should be paying attention to their work. In spite of his clear directives to the contrary, they continue to use their phones. This results in delays in answering calls, inattention to customers, the inability to focus on customers' orders, and a loss of profits from remade orders.

Managers in major corporations I have spoken with tell me they are having more and more difficulty hiring students directly out of college who possess adequate writing skills, interpersonal skills, and the ability to work effectively in groups. The new hires seemed fine as long as they could connect electronically, but personal face-to-face communication is not the same as online networking. They report that many new hires reportedly come into the workplace without a sense of boundaries, empathy, or sensitivity toward others, and many lack common respect for authority, demonstrating what is reported as a sense of entitlement.

Technology also, with its ease of information access and dissemination, allows students to have greater access to

71

methods and modes of intellectual and academic dishonesty. In conversations with teachers, I often hear of the unauthorized use of technology in schools. Several teachers indicated they've caught students texting for information during tests. Others have found students searching the Internet for answers on their cell phones, taking pictures of tests, and even loading their notes into their cell phones to access during class. In my own adult continuing education classes, when students have been instructed to only use the knowledge they possess, I'll find students searching the web for supplemental information.

A USNews.com report cited a study by San Francisco-based Common Sense Media reported that "nearly 1 in 4 students think that accessing notes on a cell phone, texting friends with answers, or using a phone to search the Internet for answers during a test isn't cheating."[46] The report also indicates that most parents (75 percent) think tech cheating occurs, but few (3 percent) can actually conceive of their own children doing it.

Plagiarism appears to be commonplace with numerous studies indicating students regularly cut and paste sections or entire text from the Internet. Teachers in my classes report students often fail to recognize that the information on the Internet is not public domain material. According to Plagiarism.org, 40 to 60 percent of students admit to having engaged in some sort of plagiarism.[47] It indicated entire passages or whole papers have been lifted from

---

[46] Zach Miners, "One Third of Teens Use Cellphones to Cheat in School," accessed April 22, 2013, *U.S. News.* http://www.usnews.com/education/blogs/on-education/2009/06/23/one-third-of-teens-use-cellphones-to-cheat-in-school

[47] plagiarism.org, accessed June 10, 2013. http://www.plagiarism.org/

the Internet and pasted into submitted documents. What many of these individuals don't realize is there is now software available to identify plagiarism and catch those who cheat. A new study by the University of Missouri found that 36 percent of students indicated that cheating was justifiable. The most common form of cheating was plagiarism, with the majority of students indicating it was done accidentally.[48]

This brings up numerous issues for businesses, from hiring individuals who have not actually completed the degree requirements to having individuals on staff who lack a moral and ethical compass to not only do things right but the right thing. How will individuals ever work through tough problems if they are only used to finding shortcuts and minimal solutions to confronting problems?

The ability to communicate effectively is being hampered in multiple ways due to the overreliance on electronic communication and the tolerance for inaccuracy attributed to text and instant messaging. With many elementary schools no longer teaching penmanship, handwritten communication may become a thing of the past.

I recently received an email invitation from the secretary of a professional statewide association asking me to speak at a large conference. I greatly appreciated the offer, but the inclusion of text language sprinkled throughout the email took me aback. I actually had to call this young lady and ask her what several of her abbreviations meant. It doesn't matter to me if this is a

---

[48] Scott Martindale, "1 in 3 Students Say Cheating Can Be Justified," accessed April 22, 2013, http://www.MSNBC.com. http://www.ocregister.com/news/cheating-295332-students-study.html

state association or business. This is not a formal business communication.

With a decreased focus on spelling and accuracy, I anticipate businesses having to waste time checking and rechecking correspondence for clarity, spelling, and sentence structure. Because of what I'm hearing from college instructors, it leads me to believe that many students are coming into class unable to form sentences and write coherently. A community college where I provide some courses for a state university has started an extensive series of college prep courses in cooperation with the local high school that prepare incoming freshman because so many are starting their college careers totally unprepared to write at an appropriate level.

Unfortunately, many of the educational issues discussed in this chapter can be pointed back to our society's mass utilization of and dependence on technology.

# 9

# Turning It Around

We may now better understand the problems related to technology overuse, misuse, and dependence, but the question still remains: what are we going to do about it?

This question is raised almost every time I speak at conferences or to any group of parents, teachers, business leaders, or health-care professionals. There are many difficulties in addressing this issue because technology is so pervasive and culturally supported. So let's break it down into bites (no pun intended) so we can address the issues without feeling like we are choking.

The first question I usually get from parents and teachers after I speak is, "Now what do I do about it?" This is why I love speaking to young people before they have children or to parents of preschool and elementary school children. Most problems, when addressed before they start, can be kept to a minimum. Many parents tell me that they wish they knew then what they know now. For young people having children or those with young children, it's important to realize the fact that modeling good behavioral patterns is essential.

As a parent, one of the best ways to begin developing more positive habits in children and adolescents is to begin modeling them yourself. Children learn by what you do, not just by what you say. Much of our learning is accomplished through watching what others do. As a parent, your role modeling sends a far more consistent and powerful message than that of any lecture or parent sit-down.

Whether they want to be or not, parents are role models. I feel that, when we take on the decision to have children, we give up the right to do whatever we want to and we must take on the role of helping our children to maximize their potential. If we don't want to take care of them, then we shouldn't have them, or we should at least allow someone who wants them to adopt and raise them. Having worked in both the addiction and child maltreatment arenas, I am still amazed at how casual some parents are about parenting. Parenting is serious work!

Self-reflection is one area where I find many parents have difficulty. It's not easy to look at yourself critically because it might mean you need to change some aspect of your own habits and behaviors. But if you knew it would have a positive, long-term impact on your child's life, wouldn't it be worth it? I recall the struggles I had as a young parent when I realized my smoking or drinking might actually increase the likelihood that my kids might influence them to do the same. It was a very tough decision to quit, but it was certainly worth it, and I have no regrets.

In my workshops, teachers and parents often ask when the right time is to start talking to their kids about _____, and then they mention one of a whole variety of social issues. I can honestly tell you (and my wife will verify it) that I began talking to our kids in utero. I have no idea if they were able to hear me or not, but from that time on, I felt it was important to speak with them about health, expectations, how great they will be, and basic predictions for positive outcomes for their lives. In their formative years, we provided them with the structure, values, and beliefs that will drive them for the rest of their lives.

## Talk to Them!

Recently, my wife and I went out for dinner at one of our favorite restaurants, the Cheesecake Factory. We order salads so we can rationalize and justify fully enjoying dessert. With over twenty-five years of dealing with various dysfunctional behaviors, I learned to rationalize with the best of them.

As we were sitting there reviewing our menus, a young couple came in with a child approximately three years old. My wife and I are always envious of young couples because our children are grown and we both really miss the noise and fingerprinted walls. It's something you don't realize you miss until they're grown.

We watched as they settled into their seats, and then I saw the mother place the child into the highchair and immediately pull a DVD player out of her bag and place it in front him. During their meal, he watched the DVD, and the parents had very little interaction with the child. I certainly don't fault the parents for wanting to have a bit of time to talk, but the DVD player stayed in front of this child during the entire meal, with little to no conversation between the child and the parents.

According to the Academy of Pediatrics and the Committee on Public Education, there are specific things parents can do related to children, adolescence, and media.[49] First, they recommend that children under two years of age should not be in front of a television. Time in front of all media (television viewing included) should not exceed an hour or two per day for younger children. If young children are exposed to television, it should be in short durations and limited to public television-type programming.

Yet how many times do parents and caretakers place children in front of the television as a substitute babysitter? Encouraging creative and interactive play, talking and having conversation with them, teaching and singing songs with them, reading stories to them, or having them read (yes, even before they are really able to read) all promote brain function development. In *Video Games & Your Kids*, Hilarie Cash and Kim McDaniel go even further and suggest that children not be exposed to "computer technology" until at least age seven.[50] This gives the brain a chance to develop within an enriched environment of love, environmental exploration, and age-appropriate stimulation.

Mealtimes are a prime opportunity for parents to model appropriate and positive interactions. Yet how many times do you see families out to dinner where every child is either texting, sitting with their phones in hand, listening to their iPods, or playing with handheld video games? Parents would be extremely wise to set boundaries on technology use by not allowing computers, iPods, phones, and other electronic devices to be used at or even brought to the table.

---

[49] Miriam E. Baron, MD, et al. "Children, Adolescents, and Television," *Pediatrics* 107 (2) (2001): 423–426.

[50] M. A. McDaniel Cash, PhD, "Video Games and Your Kids," *Issues Press* (2008), 60. http://www.videogamesandyourkids.com/

Is a family meal really a family meal if those at the table are not present due to the distractions of technology? When kids bring electronic devices, whether they are cell phones or text devices, to the table, they are not attending to the conversation; nor are they learning the norms of social interaction. There are loads of skills, abilities, and values children should learn at the table. Etiquette, social behavior, sharing, interacting, patience, the art of conversation, attending to others, and roles and responsibilities are all modeled and practiced during a family meal. These learning opportunities are lost when electronics are brought to the table.

In addition to properly modeling appropriate behavior, parents should also evaluate their own technology use. Begin by monitoring your own time spent watching TV and video clips on the computer and your general use of technology. Turn off the TV during meals with your family and discuss news stories of the day or what's new in your children's lives or otherwise show interest in others.

For the past several years, studies from Columbia University show a direct link between the number of meals you eat with your kids and their level of potential drug and alcohol use.[51] Pay attention to them during meals and in social gatherings. These times provide a great opportunity to learn about what's important to your children and to inquire about their values, goals, or thoughts on the topics of the day.

---

[51] The National Center on Addiction and Substance Abuse at Columbia University, "The Importance of Family Dinners VIII," September 2012. http://www.casacolumbia.org/addiction-research/reports/importance-of-family-dinners-2012

To help families to improve their communication, I've developed a hierarchy to consider whenever you are going to interact: face-to-face, videoconferencing, phone, letter, email, and text messaging.

- The first form of communication to consider whenever you are going to communicate is always face-to-face communication. This way, you get the opportunity to see the other person, his body language, the way he reacts, and his facial cues. For children, this is especially valuable for them to learn how to interpret what they see and respond appropriately to it. This is where mealtimes, floor time (actual time spent playing on the floor with a child), family outings, and discussions with a wide variety of individuals are so important. It takes years for individuals to become astute at reading the subtleties of interpersonal interaction. Numerous research studies show that those children who spend time in face-to-face interactions build vocabulary, learn how to adjust to changing social situations, and function better in interpersonal interactions.
- In videoconferencing, you can see the person, his environment, and the context of your conversation. I had a videoconference one Saturday morning with one of my daughters while she was living in Vancouver and I was in New Jersey. In the course of our conversation, she said she was doing well, but I could see from her body language and her reactions that something was not quite right. Seeing these things gave me the opportunity to

ask her if she were okay. As a result, she was able to tell me about a troubling incident that had occurred at her worksite that caused her a great deal of concern over the last several days. Without seeing her, I may never have known about the incident and how much it had troubled her. We were able to talk through it, and I shared some of my experiences with her that she stated were helpful in reacting to the situation. Videoconferencing today is relatively inexpensive and available to almost anyone who has a computer. Software is available free of charge, making this a very realistic form of communication for most individuals.

• The next best option is a phone call. You are able to hear the person's voice, his reactions, periods of silence, and background context that can give you a rich interaction unattainable in lesser forms of communication. In a phone call, you are often able to hear shifts in attitude, vocal tone, and tempo of speech. Each of these elements gives us valuable information into interaction as it occurs. We can often hear questions and emotions in the silence on the other end of the phone, providing us with more information than any emoticon can ever give us.

• Letters are the next best option for communication. When is the last time you received a handwritten letter from anyone? I often hear from individuals that I write letters to telling me that this is the first time they've received anything handwritten in years. Writing allows you to carefully express yourself, allowing for time afterward to reflect as to whether this is really what you wanted to say. It also gives you the opportunity to put it into an envelope, put a stamp and return address on it, and take it out to the PO box, only to retrieve it an hour later if you decide that it is not the best thing to be sending. With electronic communication today, there is most often no buffer among the emotion, writing, and sending. We think and feel something, we write it, we send it, and we regret it. I can't tell you how many organizations today that I work with that tell me this is one of the most significant problems they are dealing with. Make it a habit to never write and send an email or text message when too hungry, angry, lonely, or tired. Cursive writing has even been discontinued in many schools, with the rationale that people just don't write anymore. I want to ask, "Did it provide any benefit to developing hand-eye coordination, finite motor skills, or emotional release for someone involved in the physical act of writing?" In the absence of electronics, how will you communicate if you can't talk? Handwriting holds a myriad of benefits. It promotes logical thinking, teaches the importance of form and structure, invites creativity, and provides opportunities to experience delayed gratification through forethought, planning, and revisions.

- The next best forms of communication would be email and then text messaging. Both are highly valuable forms of communication allowing us to interact in real time, exchange information and documents, arrange meetings, and instantaneously interact in numerous other ways. For business purposes, they are now essential. I could not operate my business without them. However, there are limitations to their use. Information can be misunderstood and often is. When this occurs, individuals often try to correct the problem by using the same form of communication that got them into the problem the first place. Emotions are difficult to convey in email and text messages.

In the development of relationships, those relationships that start and proceed with an interpersonal relationship and are maintained by email and text messages seem to work fairly well. But relationships that begin and are carried on electronically often run into problems. This is often due to the fact that online relationships oftentimes do not prepare you adequately to carry on an interpersonal connection.

Strong interpersonal relationships that exist over extended periods of time require those four elements of time, testing, tenacity, and triumph. It takes time and patience to really get to know another person. Relationships are complicated. There are times when you hit rough spots, and you must have the tenacity to work through them. Strong relationships also need shared experiences and time dedicated to celebrate their achievements. That is why anniversaries are important milestones to be celebrated. I'm sure this happens to some extent online, but it is the exception and not what I hear or see as the norm.

## Model Appropriate Behavior

In addition to teaching the importance of face-to-face communication, parents also need to model the behaviors they want to see in their children. Read books to set the reading example. Books enhance creative thinking and build skills they will use a lifetime. Reading to a child enhances bonding between the parent and the child, encouraging positive interaction. Allowing the child to read the book back to the parent also encourages mastery of skills, encouraging continued skill development.

Use the TV (for children over two years of age) and the TV or computer (for children over five years of age) in limited amounts and for short durations as rewards in combination with face time activities. This is done rather than taking them away from children as a form of punishment. Removal for negative behavior only elevates technology's value in their lives because we tend to want the things that are forbidden.

Until children are in high school, don't put a computer or TV in their bedroom. This encourages social isolation and removes your ability to monitor what they watch. You can model appropriate media exposure by monitoring how your children use the technology around them. The TV shows you allow your children and adolescents to watch should be quality programming and not that which seems to glamorize, advocate, and model misbehavior. When you allow your children to watch television, watch it with them to monitor the content. When it is inappropriate for them, change the channel or turn it off and talk with them about it. Engage your children in important discussions, and teach them the value of critical thinking.

Also, please use discretion in the kind of content you allow your children and adolescents to be exposed to. I have had numerous teachers and social workers tell me stories of children speaking to them about very adult subjects they have seen late in the evening while watching TV with their parents.

If programming comes on that is controversial or has questionable content around sexual conduct, violent behavior, drugs, or your family values and if the child is of appropriate age, use the subject matter for discussion on what is appropriate, moral, legal, ethical, valued, and right. When the content is violent and gruesome, parents need to be aware that, "The results show that both the frequency of play and affinity for violent games were strongly associated with delinquent and violent behavior," as Craig Anderson, professor of psychology and director of the Center for the Study of Violence at Iowa State, reported.[52]

Please notice that I said the TV programs that you allow them to watch. As a parent, it's important to take control of the television and media. You pay the electric bill. More than likely, you also bought the television, computer, cell phone, DVD player, music player, tablet computer, or many of the other technologies available to them.

Selectively promote and make available high-quality programming that is educational, stimulates creative thinking, fosters exploration, and furthers learning. Young people need guidance and clear boundaries in order to develop a sense of balance in their lives, values, beliefs, and behavior. They also need to learn how to develop the proper balance in the use of technologies. One of the ways children can learn this balance is

---

[52] "Violent Video Games Are a Risk Factor for Criminal Behavior and Aggression, New Evidence Shows," accessed June 12, 2013, *Science Daily*. http://www.sciencedaily.com/releases/2013/03/130326121605.htm

by observing how you as their parent model appropriate behavior. Encourage children to seek alternatives.

Entertainment technology is amazing! From our widescreen TVs to our ability to watch movies on flights or listen to music almost anywhere, technology provides incredible opportunities. And to truly see what Disney and Pixar have done is remarkable. *Avatar* is the only movie I have paid for that I saw three times in the movie theater.

In the right place, for the right reasons, for the right person, and in the right balance, technology is fantastic. But when it becomes overwhelming, hazardous, stressful, compulsive, and counterproductive, we need to take a serious look at it. Numerous studies show that children raised and educated in enriched environments learn better and have enhanced brain development. We learn best when we have a variety of experiences that engage all of our senses and are experienced in multiple ways.[53] Providing multiple options for learning gives everyone the opportunity to experience information at different levels and in her own way.

When information is provided in multiple venues, this offers novelty and various ways for our brains to gather the information. This stimulates the development of creativity as well as the enhancement of critical thinking. Learning in multiple forms allows the learner to feel the experience, see the process as it unfolds into the finished product, and hear the interaction with others.

---

[53] Eric Jensen, *Brain-Based Learning: The New Paradigm of Teaching*, 2nd ed. (Thousand Oaks, Calif.: Corwin Press, 2008), 193. http://www.amazon.com/Brain-Based-Learning-The-Paradigm-Teaching/dp/1412962560

Parents can model appropriate behavior by encouraging their kids to tune into the world and all it has to offer. And yet, it's amazing to me how disconnected we have become. Take your child out for a walk in the park or woods, go fishing with her, discover a museum together, build a blanket and chair fort, or volunteer in the community together. Engage in new experiences that you and your family can enjoy together.

We have disconnected from society as many individuals no longer take part in community groups, religious activities, and cultural/social events. We have also detached ourselves through our disuse of public transportation. All you need to do is drive down any interstate highway and notice how many cars have only one person in them.

Organizations have become disconnected through the fact that email and texting are sometimes taking the place of staff meetings and normal workplace interactions. Gossip is no longer primarily exchanged at the water cooler. Now, it is much more likely to be read through some social networking site.

Families have disconnected from each other as they sit together watching television without much interaction, if any at all. At the dinner table, it is not uncommon to see individuals, even in restaurants, together texting other people or listening to their music on headphones. And even going to a school play or children's sporting event, it's interesting to watch how many parents are totally present and how many are reading, texting, calling, or disconnecting from the event through some electronic device. With all of this technological stimulation, do children today even get the opportunity to learn how to silently pray, meditate, or otherwise make the most of a few minutes of silence in their lives? Are parents even modeling these behaviors for their children?

There's something to be said for sitting quietly and listening to others at the table talk about family history, share family stories, and discuss what the elders think. Are we robbing some of the wisdom derived from the observation of conversations and being surrounded by the values of the family and community?

Technology is great, but it's just as important to turn it off periodically with regular and extended blackout periods. How else would someone learn to be creative, self-reliant, and inquisitive? During weather-related blackouts over the past couple years, parents report that they and their children had no idea what to do without electric and their electronic devices. Parents can model appropriate behavior by learning the value of quiet or idle time, telling stories to help build their children's vocabulary and their ability to visualize, and providing creative activities they can do when there is "nothing to do."

I was amazed today to find out that many young people have no idea how to use a card catalog or do research using real books and periodicals. Not all old behaviors are antiquated. Teach your children how to do research in multiple forms. Make books available for those who want them, whether they're on printed paper or e-book format. E-readers are great, but I believe it's important to learn to also really use books. For books that you own, write in the margins, underline passages, bend down the corners, and appreciate the work that went into the writing. Unfortunately, this may be becoming a lost art.

When children pretend to read, they are getting ready to read so encourage them to "read" to you even before they are capable of actually doing so. Besides, you'll be amazed as they retell the story from the perceptions they have and what they get out of it. If you are going to include technology as part of their entertainment, try coupling it with the reading of the book and possibly discussing the difference between the movie and the book. As soon as they are capable, encourage them to write their own stories, and let them read them to you and draw pictures to illustrate the stories they create.

Encourage all types of creative play. Years ago when our children were small, I would take a piece of paper and draw stick figures on it to inspire creativity. We would draw stick figure horses, people, and anything else we could imagine to create villages, castles, and anything you could think of. I would then give them scissors to cut out the stick figures, allowing enough room around them to create small "wings" at the base of each figure that could be bent around to the back, allowing them to stand. Once I drew the figures and they figured out how to play this type of activity, they often would play with these small paper figures for hours.

Play is important at every age. Over the past several years, I have used small plastic blocks in almost every training session and meeting I have facilitated. Initially, I wasn't certain how adults would take to them; however, after a second meeting where people requested them, I knew I was on to something. Now I consistently put stress balls, small blocks, or other small toys on the tables in front of the attendees for them to manipulate. It is wonderful to see a staff meeting or boardroom with adults sitting and discussing serious topics while manipulating blocks. The use of manipulatives helps to internally process the information being working with and actually enhances the ability to maintain focused attention. I encourage parents or teachers to consider this technique for use during class or while studying. Not all participants, children or adults, want or can handle manipulatives on their desks so use your judgment when considering their use.

Parents can encourage their children to be creative by modeling important and valuable behaviors such as reading, visualization, playing, and silent thinking, prayer, or meditation.

## Mind Mapping

Mind mapping is an excellent creative exercise for gathering information, brainstorming, going through strategic planning, and handling a myriad of other tasks that are normally done using the same old boring formats. Mind mapping involves the collection of data in a dynamic form that allows for interpretation, shows relationships, and increases memory of not only the process but also the specifics within it. And it accommodates numerous learning and interpretive styles.

Mind mapping starts with the diagramming of a central idea and is then followed by branching off that central idea into various subcategories, forming an "information map" that replicates the way we think and learn. When the mind map is completed, it can look very chaotic to an outside observer. But for the person or group developing it, it shows streams of thought, idea relationships, and concept areas in a highly visual form that enhances recall.

Ideas and thoughts can be recorded in words, pictures, or anything that has meaning to the person constructing the mind map. Below is a mind map for a course I was developing on public speaking. Note that the colors separate idea streams while helping me to visualize the flow of how I might present this information.

Mind maps can be created by hand or with various forms of software. One of my favorite pieces of software is from Inspiration. com. Schools all over use it for educational purposes. For those who learn and process information differently (maybe you or your children), this can be a valuable tool.

On the next page is a mind map created using Inspiration Mind Mapping software for a course on public speaking. Note how the separate idea streams link thoughts to the central idea and then branch out to include secondary and tertiary ideas.

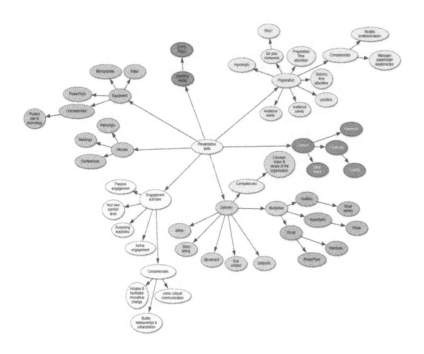

**Mind map created using Inspiration®**

As a young person, I struggled tremendously with reading, English, math, and numerous subjects requiring linear thinking. It wasn't until my own kids were going to school that I realized I wasn't unintelligent; I just learned differently than most people. In my wildest dreams, I never thought I'd write anything anyone would want to read, but when I discovered mind mapping, everything changed. When I developed the concepts for my first book, *The Pond: A Small Book about Making Big Changes*, I knew I needed to find a better way to organize multiple streams of thought. Outlines just don't work for me. With *The Pond*, I wanted to offer a written resource capable of helping organizations and families navigate the tumultuous waters of change. I utilized mind mapping to prepare and write *The Pond*.[54] Mind mapping helped me write my very first book.

In researching this technique, I found Tony Buzan's numerous books very helpful. I would suggest a small paperback he wrote, *Use Both Sides of Your Brain*,[55] as it provided a great deal of information about different types of learning clear examples on how the maps can be used.

There are numerous samples for you to review on the Internet as well as resources on how to develop written mind maps or even electronic versions. I also utilize the relatively inexpensive (around $70), downloadable software from Inspiration that created my

---

[54] This resource is available at http://krigerconsulting.com/resources.html, and it provides the reader with the ten deceptively simple elements needed to navigate through change. http://krigerconsulting.com/resources.html

[55] Tony Buzan, *Use Both Sides of Your Brain: New Mind-Mappinh Techniques* (New York: Penguin Books, 1991). http://www.amazon.com/Use-Both-Sides-Your-Brain/dp/0452266033

previous model.[56] It is simple to use and easy to learn, and I've interacted with the company on numerous occasions where they have been very helpful with technical assistance.[57]

Mind mapping organizes thoughts without forcing you into a linear process. It can be as dynamic, colorful, and messy as you would like or as linear as necessary. The nice part about the Inspiration software is that, once you create a mind map, all you need to do is hit one button and it automatically puts it into a linear outline. This works very well for individuals who are nonlinear thinkers.

I have to admit, though, that my favorite way to mind map is with a large sheet of paper up on the wall and utilizing markers, crayons, tape, and pictures to create a visual representation of everything regarding the topic at hand. I have used this method and seen outstanding results with corporations and leadership groups in numerous sessions I have facilitated. It's extremely exciting to see a group of adults set free to create ideas they would like to see in the future orchestrated on paper through markers, crayons, and tape. Try it at you next creative session or staff meeting!

---

[56] Inspiration Software, Inc., accessed April 22, 2013. (Vendor pays no endorsement fee or remuneration for this recommendation.) http://www.inspiration.com/

[57] I do not receive an endorsement fee from either Tony Buzan or Inspiration, but I am a genuine believer in the resources mentioned. As a result, I wanted to include them in my manual as additional resources for parents and other interested readers.

## The Power of Imagination

Many of the individuals I speak with today in management positions are finding it hard to hire college graduates who are good at creative problem-solving, abstract thinking, and the generation of multiple solutions to complex problems. To address this issue, I'm currently working on a training session, "Imagination 101." Imagination games, group challenges, and thought-change exercises are great for increasing creativity and building brainpower. While some people will take the course, you can begin enhancing your own level of creativity right at home.

When our family went on vacation, someone in the car would pick two totally unrelated objects and ask the rest of us to come up with as many ideas as we could within two to three minutes as to how those two objects were similar. The requirement of the game is to come up with as many things as you can within the time limit, whether they make sense or not. This game emphasizes quantity over quality. The more answers you can come up with, the better chance of winning. Your answers don't have to make sense. It's doing the exercise and learning to allow things to be said, as well as accepting someone else's answers without censoring. Try doing this after dinner or when you are in the car. The more you practice it, the more likely you will start to become more effective in doing it.

As parents, we can encourage our children to cultivate vivid imaginations. Today, I use this exercise as a team-building activity in many of my workshops. It's amazing how many of the groups are initially very hesitant and censor themselves from saying anything that doesn't make sense. But once the competition gets going, all sorts of ridiculous and nonsensical responses are provided.

This elicits laughter and builds trust between members. This trust is built because, in order to have a chance of winning, you need to get comfortable quickly with each other, believing that the other person will accept what you have to say and that he will support you at a time when you feel less than perfect. Motivated to win, both of you have to trust each other. It's very encouraging to watch a group do this early in the day as guarded, hesitant, cautious people, only to see them later in the session carrying on and getting crazy. This activity is great for family game time or kicking off a staff meeting or planning session because it helps all those involved develop the power of their imaginations.

## The Importance of Physical Activity

Encouraging physical activity provides stimulation to different areas of the brain. This provides experiences that balance out the needs of your nervous and physical systems to maintain health and proper functioning. Without adequate practice, your capabilities may erode, impairing your ability to function properly. If a person is hospitalized for an extended period of time, it is important to try to get her up and standing so she does not lose the ability to balance, walk, and function.

As previously discussed, what you practice is enhanced, and what you ignore erodes. In some instances, extreme gamers and technology addicts have become so withdrawn and absorbed that they have neglected their children[58] or allowed pets to starve.[59] Gaming is fine when it is limited, breaks are taken during play, and time is taken to eat, drink, and go to the bathroom. But when individuals begin wearing adult diapers so they don't have to get up from the game, I believe their technology use has gotten out of control. In some cases, checking Facebook, text messages, and email in the morning is common before their feet ever hit the ground. It is important to keep balance in your life and to maintain a healthy body, and physical activity is an important aspect of maintaining that balance.

I wonder how many children and adults for that matter never get the opportunity to walk on grass, rocky shores, or silken sand or up stony inclines. Instead, they are restricted to blacktop pavement and cement. Walking on uneven surfaces stimulates various areas of the brain, improves awareness, and, if done with some frequency and duration, improves health. A physical therapist told me that walking on uneven surfaces actually enhances areas of the brain pertaining to balance. Three areas located in the cerebellum in your brain are involved with balance: vision, the vestibular system, and proprioception.

- Vision is the input you take in to recognize your relationship to your surroundings. When you strain your vision over time, it can make it harder to focus and can

---

[58] Edecio Martinez, "Mother Obsessed with Computer Game Neglects Kids, Starves Dogs," accessed April 22, 2013, *CBS News*. http://www.cbsnews.com/news/mother-obsessed-with-computer-game-neglects-kids-starves-dogs/

[59] "Online Gaming: As Destructive as a Heroin Addiction?" accessed April 22, 2013, myce. http://www.myce.com/news/online-gaming-as-destructive-as-a-heroin-addition-34601/

potentially cause vision problems. Your eyes are lubricated when you blink. An individual who stares at a computer screen for a long period of time can develop eye strain, resulting in headaches, reduced ability to focus, and dry eyes. If you practice using your vision to assess and react to different distances, weights, objects, temperatures, and other experiences you encounter, you develop the ability to judge how to approach and physically handle situations based on your prior experience of seeing these things before. But staring at a computer screen does not allow you to develop these abilities. Instead of your vision being enhanced, overuse of technology can actually strain your vision.

- Your vision helps you recognize your relationship to your surroundings. Your vestibular system is the brain structure that actually processes the orientation of where your body is in relation to your surroundings. This system keeps you upright and in proper alignment and posture. Proprioception is the developed ability within the vestibular system to know where you are in relation to your surroundings and to move your body with the appropriate amount of force and movement to put a bottle of milk in the refrigerator or to reach down to pick up your child. It relays information regarding the space you are in and where things are in relation to your movements.

When you are walking on an uneven surface, this portion of the brain tells your body to move and react in relation to the changing terrain. Practicing movement in different circumstances enhances these abilities. However when you stay in one position too long or fail to experience a range of physical movements within varied environments, you may actually lose the ability to do so. When you consider the physical inactivity many individuals experience when using technology to extremes, it is a wonder they can even walk and navigate varied surroundings when they encounter them.

There are numerous benefits to physical activity that you can get without running marathons and buying thousand pounds of weights. You want to strive for a balance between your sedentary activities on the computer and some physical activity. Ideally, getting up to stretch, walk around, and rehydrate at least every hour would be great, but for many, this is just not happening.

By moving, you increase the oxygen levels to your body and brain. Toxins that build up with inactivity are released. Muscles are stimulated and used, keeping your body strong. Your brain is synchronized with your movements. With inactivity, muscles weaken, as does your posture. According to one study, kids' posture went into the common slouched position with five minutes of playing computer games: head forward, shoulders rounded, and back in a forward bent position.[60] According to my discussions with physical therapist Genevieve Beasock, "This may very well create neck, back, arm, and leg pain later in life. Their breathing is also restricted, reducing oxygen levels as they play."[61]

---

[60] Jason Kotowski, "No Slouching! Study Examined Posture While Playing Video Games," accessed April 22, 2013, *The Bakersfield Californian.* http://www.bakersfieldcalifornian.com/local/x1008890001/No-slouching-Study-examined-posture-while-playing-video-games

[61] Genevieve Beasock, personal interview, 2012.

Exercise doesn't have to entail a lot of time or even energy. Getting up from the computer screen every forty-five minutes or every hour and stretching would be a move in the right direction. Go downstairs and get a glass of water, do a few toe touches, or just walk around the house or office. Movement reinvigorates the body and wakes up the mind. The National Football League realizes the importance of movement and has taken on a program called NFL 60, promoting sixty minutes a day of physical activity along with improved eating.[62]

New research indicates that sitting for long periods of time puts us all at risk. Some schools and offices are actually using standing desks in order to increase circulation and movement and decrease obesity. In my personal office, I have made a partial transition and am currently investigating how to convert my desk into a standing desk. After two weeks of experimenting with it, I can say I like it. I move more, sit less, and find that I am actually less tired at the end of the day. (Of course, a few short breaks are good during the day.)

Yoga and Tai Chi are other wonderful approaches to exercise that are relatively stress-free. They take very little time and can be done without any equipment. They also help to balance the mind and the body, offsetting much of the stress we experience from computer use, especially online gaming.

I often hear from parents and teachers that many young people have no idea what to do when there's nothing to do. Think about encouraging your kids to become involved in various organized and pickup sports. Take them hiking, rock

---

[62] National Dairy Council and NFL, *Fuel Up to Play 60.* http://www.fueluptoplay60.com/

climbing, kayaking, and canoeing, or build tree forts in wooded areas or sand castles at the beach with them. Boxes are great for constructing forts at home.

Encourage the use of paper, blankets, small tables, chairs, and boxes for them to experience different textures. For kids, these are all activities that increase their physical involvement, enhance their awareness of their surroundings, promote interaction with others, and may even stimulate team building. Physical activity helps promote movement, which can help safeguard against a primary health problem in America today, obesity.

## Find a Hobby, and Learn Life Skills

Like physical activity, exposing children and young people to hobbies can help to increase focused attention and also reduce stress. Many hobbies can be done at little or no cost. Other hobbies may require a minimal investment but can often yield maximum results.

For several years, I made many of the gifts I gave to others by teaching myself the art of leather carving and stamping. Many items can be made from scraps of leather or can be purchased in small kits. This can often be done with a minimal investment and can expand as far as you would like to take it. For some individuals I know, leatherworking has grown from a hobby into a full-time business. During my involvement in leatherworking, I undertook numerous small projects in addition to becoming far more involved in larger projects like designing and hand-sewing briefcases and other large items.

Numerous books, CDs, and videos on the Internet will help teach your kids how to become involved in different crafts and hobbies. Sometimes, I think it's worthwhile just exposing children and youth to a variety of activities because it gives them options for consideration and later involvement. Not only do these hobbies reduce stress and enhance their creativity, focus, and concentration, they can also open their eyes to possibilities for future careers and interests. Not everything that is worthwhile comes with an on/off switch.

Classes are available in many after-school programs or through the library, YMCA, and other governmental or nonprofit agencies. Exploring music, painting, sculpting, and building all enhance creativity and build social structures while teaching your children valuable interpersonal skills that will last a lifetime.

Oftentimes, these hobbies work to instill a sense of confidence and identity within our children. This confidence translates into important life skills and interpersonal interactions. Those better able to read and accurately respond to nonverbal communications will be more effective than those lacking these skills. Being able to establish eye contact, engage in empathetic listening, interpret responses of others, react to nonverbal cues, and engage in conversation are all personal skills necessary to manage relationships, get ahead in school, and find and progress in a job.

Balancing a checkbook, preparing meals, doing laundry, and paying taxes are life skills, which young people are often reportedly lacking. To be able to network effectively, it is necessary to know how to dine out with the proper etiquette so you can feel confident enough to meet and interact socially. These skills often differentiate those who succeed from those who don't.

If we allow ourselves and our children to become obsessed with technology, our lives will be missing the richness and vitality of true interpersonal relationships. Therefore, we need to be consciously and actively seek to build the skills necessary to live life well with others.

## Connect through Real FaceTime

Many of us know that Apple has revolutionized the concept of face time, but I would suggest parents spend more face-to-face time truly communicating with their young people. Even providing opportunities for multigenerational sharing helps to develop patience, listening skills, and hopefully appreciation for the wisdom of different experiences and ages.

As I discussed earlier, face-to-face communication allows for the sharing of perceptions and refining of self-image and personal values. As children become older, many parents have the misperception that their children need them less. My experience is just the opposite, and I believe that, as our children get older, the challenges they face are greater so they actually need us more. The attention we provide to them is different, but the importance of their decisions is greater.

Face-to-face interactions give us the opportunity to find out what other people want, need, and think about. This gives individuals an opportunity to expand their thinking as differing opinions expose them to different belief systems and methods for problem-solving and living life. This is different than the information you would receive on the computer because you actually have the opportunity to observe the person as he is talking.

Developing empathy and listening skills is a huge benefit to those who more effectively relate and respond to others in person. Unless you are using videoconferencing, these skills are very difficult to develop via the computer because the isolation of the computer screen and the distancing of the person on the other side depersonalize the interaction.

Interpersonal face-to-face communication requires that both sides intend to communicate with integrity. How many times have you felt disregarded while talking to someone on the telephone when you could hear the click of his computer keys in the background, knowing that he is speaking to you but doing something else at the same time?

You can feel when someone is not present, but this is often the type of interaction that occurs through electronic media. I could easily tell when my daughter was distracted when my wife and I would call her for a status report. We would get one-word responses or numerous requests to repeat our questions because she was so busy on the computer or watching television. And more than likely, it was a combination of the two.

Attending to the needs of others enhances relationships when you are focused on the other person by making him important in the interaction. But when he is treated as an intruder, an interrupter, or a secondary concern, it actually damages the relationship by communicating that the other person is not as important as the other things you are doing.

How many relationships have suffered because one person was distracted and not valuing the other person he is with or talking to? When you are competing with something else, you certainly don't feel as if the person you are with is valuing you in the interaction and you know you are not his top priority. Computer use, though, is often so engaging and enticing that priorities are often misplaced.

Learning to prioritize and manage tasks is a huge undertaking for many individuals currently enamored by and compulsively involved in technology and gaming. There is great value in learning to stop, pray, or meditate. Discover yourself and the serenity life can offer through meditation, mindfulness, or even walking a labyrinth.

Each summer, I teach several courses in which I provide a segment on walking a labyrinth, a centuries-old walking meditation path used by many to relax, recover, work through issues, find solace, and, more recently, act as a therapeutic or team-building exercise. Labyrinths are found around the world in parks, churches, retreat and treatment centers, and hospitals, to name but a few areas.

Many individuals who struggle with traditional meditation find this form very easy to learn and do because you don't have to be still. There is really no wrong or right way to walk it as long as you treat it—and those walking on the labyrinth as well—with respect. Recognize that this is a semi-sacred space to many, so keep that in mind if you try walking one.

The experience and skills you can learn by exploring these and other approaches to silence, prayer, or meditation can enrich and add a dimension of peace to your life. These types of meditation also offset the constant stress of life and technology use, putting you in touch with yourself and the world around you. They help you to recharge and refocus, effectively enabling you to be more directed and present in your interpersonal relationships.

As a young person wanting to understand others more, I spent years studying psychology, sociology, organizational behavior, addictive behavior, and a whole host of other approaches. Yet, instead of seeking to understand others better, today many individuals seem to strive to disconnect from those around them. As we have been discussing in this manual, technology provides a means by which people can disconnect from their surrounding environment.

At times, I have even noticed myself becoming more and more disconnected from my wife, kids, and myself. And I have noticed I am not the only one. The economy has gotten us all concerned to the point where we work harder, with most of us knowing someone who has lost a job, is struggling in his job, or is experiencing tension, anxiety, or depression because of the economy.

So we work harder to make up for the losses we have taken, or we try to create more work for ourselves to reassure ourselves and our families. All the while, we struggle to create more stability in our lives because of a lack of true security in our jobs. For many, technology can be a way to develop a false sense of security or at least distract someone from the struggles of real life.

After my mom died in January 2011, I disconnected from many of the people I love. Maybe it was out of fear of eventually losing them as well or knowing I am getting older. Or maybe it's just because I didn't know how to deal with my mom's death. At times, I've even disconnected from myself, not wanting to feel all that life has to offer because it just sometimes seems like too much to handle. And then, I remember that life is an experience to be felt. Each event that happens provides you an option of how you want to experience it. If you disconnect, you miss that moment in life and can never get it back. After having two life events where I didn't know if I would live or not, I've learned that I don't want to miss even one moment. I want and need to connect with myself, my family, my friends, and my life.

Good things pass, but so does the pain we endure. The secret is to connect and to stay connected to whatever is happening in your life. Each breath you take is a new breath, one you have never taken in the way you are taking it right now. It really is the breath of life that we so often take for granted. See those around you, and know that each moment with them is a gift and an opportunity to connect with them. Connecting allows us to be more fully human and to share in the life that others walk.

So, today, this week, or maybe even this month, try joining me in connecting. It's your life. Don't miss a minute of it. To balance ourselves in this age of technology is essential so we can learn to relax, clear our minds, and reduce the clutter of constantly being "on." Our technology has off switches, but many times, we don't even give ourselves the chance to rest and recharge.

## Boundaries, Routines, and Responsible Stewardship

Setting up routines that allow for time on the computer and time to relax and socialize is an important endeavor in order to balance today's overactive lifestyles. Boundaries need to be set so that there are times when we are not available to others. There is almost a sense today that, if you were to lose contact through your cell phone or computer, you would cease to exist.

Many individuals years ago would be found walking down the street with a large radio on their shoulder, blasting music in an attempt to resolve their invisibility and feelings of meaningless. Today, all you need to do is go into a chat room, post a belief, or send out a tweet, and you will have numerous responses. You can have almost instant significance as a result of today's technology.

For some, the Internet is a wonderful place to meet people, share ideas, and interact with speed and ease. Housebound seniors can now interact with each other and their families, improving their moods and helping them to sustain themselves despite being in a physically imposed isolation. Individuals with disabilities are able to have their needs met and develop high levels of social interaction that were never before possible.

Idea sharing has gone global, enhancing all of us in our thinking and realization of possibilities. Social networking sites have helped family members connect, long-lost relatives find each other, and even adopted children find their birth parents. In some instances, miraculous stories have arisen out of contacts made, sustained, and nurtured through the use of social networking. The capacity of our electronic communications has only begun to be realized.

At the same time, numerous research articles and books indicate the Internet is often a place where individuals struggling with interpersonal relationships and social interaction turn to. Unfortunately, their use of the Internet further isolates them while enhancing their sense of community and intimacy in relationships.

As a result, individuals are spending more time in their cyber relationships than they are with real people in interpersonal interactions. Because we tend to build skills in areas of our experience, these individuals lack the experience of interpersonal interactions and may very well lose the ability to develop intimate relationships with depth and integrity. This can only be addressed through increasing physical interaction. By engaging in social activities, participating in groups, and taking responsibility for understanding and being understood, you begin to improve the integrity of your interactions.

For those individuals in recovery from alcohol or drug abuse, the computer is a gateway for relapse. It encourages isolation by the very nature of disconnection of humanity through a keyboard. Addiction offers social isolation, distancing from your feelings, acceptance within a peer group of like-minded individuals, and a freedom from taking responsibility for your actions because you can now blame it on the drug or the drink. How many of these elements are also true today in our use of technology?

Just as it is important for a drug or alcohol addict to remain connected to a support system, it is vital for those struggling with their personal identity to remain connected to those around them, not find their ultimate validation via the Internet. It is important for parents and responsible individuals to recognize the amount of responsibility involved in the use of electronic communications and technology. Great power really does come with great responsibility. Technology certainly is extremely powerful. But with that power also comes greater responsibility to steward those tools wisely.

Unfortunately, some people don't always know how to responsibly steward these tools or to set up proper boundaries in how they use technology. For some, their involvement in technology might lead them down destructive roads such as online gambling or cybersex just to name a few.

Gambling, especially online, may be fun for some, but the compulsive and reinforcing way it is provided presents a very enticing trap for many individuals in recovery. Here are some behaviors that you might look for in your loved one that might indicate a problem related to gambling:

- phone calls at all hours of the night or day
- people stopping by the house you don't know
- resistance to talk to you about or introduce you to his or her friends
- extreme nervousness on the part of your loved one when someone comes to the door or calls and asks for her

These could be signs of gambling, but they also may very well be indicators of other problems such as technology addiction. Parents need to be engaged in the lives of their children and to discuss with them the importance of boundaries and discretion in how they use the technology around them.

Another area of Internet use that parents need to be aware of is cyber seduction, an ever-present danger that many young people approach nonchalantly. Within the past week, I was told of an adolescent who was meeting men online. When her parents were not home, she was inviting them to her house and didn't see a problem with it. Many school counselors I speak with tell me students don't see a problem interacting with people online and then making arrangements without their parents' knowledge to meeting that online friend in person.

Parents need to check Internet histories and ask many of the same questions they would ask if their child were going out:

- Who are you going with? Where are you going?
- How long will you be gone? When will you return?
- Are there any adults going to be there?
- Are you going anywhere else in the time you will be gone?

The tactics of asking good questions, checking histories on the computer, or requiring the computer to be in a common area of the house are not spying on your child. Rather, it is being responsible. These tactics help your child learn the importance of boundaries and stewardship in their use of technology. This is important because, quite frankly, your children need you to establish boundaries for them. If you were to look at the development of a child's brain, you would see that, even through later adolescence, many areas of the brain are not fully developed, that is, young people very often do not make good decisions because they don't have the capacity to properly reason through the situation. It doesn't mean that they lack intelligence. As parents, we need to be vigilant longer and more often than we think.

Our children need information provided to them longer than they think they need it and in greater amounts than they want it. When you attempt to tell them something or teach them a lesson and they say, "I know. You told me before," tell them again! This is called duration and intensity. Parents need to provide support and guidance far longer than their children and adolescents think they need it. It takes time for them to take in the information and for us to make sure that information is really embedded into that actively developing brain. We also need to make sure that we talk to and are involved with them in their daily lives. Many times, this will be more often than they think they need us.

Kids need their parents' influence to develop positive attitudes, honorable values, and respectable behaviors that will serve them for the rest of their lives. If parents abdicate their responsibilities as parents, role models, and counselors, someone or something else will step in and fill that void in the child's life. Without your adequate influence, the media, society, and their peers will primarily influence your children.

With all the time spent online, in what ways are our children being influenced, and what lessons are they learning? The seduction of a perfect world created in the mind and witnessed on the screen can provide an alternative for some to abandon their day-to-day lives, choosing instead to spend more and more of their life in a virtual reality. This is especially seductive to children and adolescents who need of social development and personal interaction.

Childhood and adolescence are formative times when values, beliefs, self-image, and the development of intimacy in relationships are essential in becoming an adult. And parents often find it difficult—if not impossible—to bring themselves to set limits and boundaries on the ways their children interact with and use technology. Many fear being the only parent their child knows who doesn't allow them to _____. Here are some more helpful guidelines for parents to consider:

- Consider a weekday moratorium on television.
- Check the TV ratings and content of the shows your kids watch.

- Do the same for the computer and video games your children play.
- Recognize that, as your children grow, they need you more, not less.

A weekday moratorium on television will allow the family to sit together and watch recorded programming or to spend time in the evenings completing homework, attending different events, or playing board games. Increased interaction with family members enhances relationships and provides opportunities for children to witness appropriate adult interactions.

When children are allowed to watch television, check the ratings and content to make sure the programs teach the type of information you want your children to know. Consider utilizing screening software that many of today's televisions already have in order to protect your children from programs with extreme violence or adult language and situations.

Check computer and video game ratings and watch the game while your child plays it for the first few times. I am amazed at how many games today have multiple levels that allow you to get into more and more adult content as you go. Also be aware that older children bring games into the home, providing younger children access to those games. Older children should set an example by not choosing or not being allowed to choose extremely violent or sexually-oriented video games. Be aware that numerous studies today indicate that children who watch violent video games are often less empathetic and more prone to overreacting to peers.

The most important recommendation I can make is that, as children grow, the need for their parents is more, not less.

The decisions they make have greater impact on their lives as they grow older. We as parents need to begin as early as possible and as consistently as we can to reinforce positive values and to interact with them in just about anything we can insert ourselves into. Consider playing video games with them, watching TV and discussing the programs, and requiring that they join you in family responsibilities so they can learn what it means to engage in acceptable behavior before they leave the home.

I often hear from young people that they have no responsibilities at home, and yet when they go out on their own, they are almost totally helpless. They lack many of the skills necessary to live on their own—money management, cooking for themselves, involving themselves in social activities, and establishing positive peer groups—will help them to achieve their goals.

When young people are growing up, they need parents to be parents and not their friends. Children with high standards will fail at times, but those with no standards have little to try to attain. As a parent, you only have one opportunity to do it right, and we all need as much help as we can get. And I can tell you, no matter how hard you try, you will mess up somewhere. However, following some of the suggestions provided in this manual can greatly improve your ability to interact with your children and assist them in becoming adults with clearer values, beliefs, and behaviors coupled with balanced technology use.

# 10

# Final Thoughts

So what do you do if you are having difficulties with your technology use or you know someone who does? Here are ten helpful steps to offset the negative impact of technology abuse and dependence:

- interpersonal communication
- the art of social conversation
- making relationships work
- self-awareness (and awareness of the way you express your emotions)
- living skills
- establishing and knowing boundaries
- the art of relaxation
- creative thought
- managing emotions
- getting a life

## Step #1: Interpersonal Communication

*Listening with Heart*

With our increasing use of technology, there is a tendency to decrease face-to-face communication. While this reduction is seen as just a sign of the times, indirect human interaction may encourage us to get out of practice when communicating directly. Many individuals find it easier to text or email than to engage each other in person. Texting and email are faster and easier because they provide an opportunity to communicate simplistic information quickly and relatively effortlessly.

The problems come in when we try to convey more complex information. Texting and email are excellent forms of communication for simplistically conveying facts and sharing documents; however, there is more to communication than just the words themselves.

It's important for individuals to understand the context in which information is provided. Telling you "I understand" has meaning and conveys empathy when you see me looking at you, facing directly toward you, and hearing my voice soften. All of these cues are consistent with someone demonstrating concern and showing deliberate signs of joining emotionally in the moment. However, if I were talking with you and you were to see me looking at my watch, looking around the room at what others are doing, or fidgeting with something in my hands, you may conclude these are an indication of me being uncomfortable, distracted, or not being in touch with your emotions.

Without some context information, the intended message can be taken in whatever manner the person receiving it decides it should be. Those in the business of communications know that the context in which information is provided is often more important than the information itself. Listening is more than just hearing the words because it requires engaging the heart in the interaction.

Have you ever become frustrated in communicating electronically? How did electronic communication contribute to that frustration? How could that frustration been minimized or avoided altogether by using a combination of electronic and face-to-face communication or eliminating electronic communication altogether? What steps will you take to improve communications in your life and work?

*Speaking Effectively*

Developing the appropriate vocabulary to adequately describe your thoughts is a skill that sets many apart. Yet when these skills are either not developed or not practiced, they can diminish over time, reducing your ability to adequately and accurately convey your thoughts and meaning.

Speaking effectively means being able to understand what you want to say and having a vocabulary developed enough so you are able to have those receiving your message understand it clearly and as intended.

Are you aware of the volume, tone, and speed of speech that you and others use? Speaking too loudly can be an indication of anger while speaking too softly may convey timidity. How do others receive you? Have you ever asked? It is often advised and even acceptable to ask close friends and family how you come across. This can give you insight into your communications and provide you with valuable reflection to improve your interpersonal communications.

The only caution is to make sure you are willing to hear what someone has to say. It does no good to ask for help only to defend yourself or be defensive. People are often very willing to help when they are asked if they find what they have to say is accepted and considered.

Does your use of electronic communication stand in the way of your verbal communication skills? Think back to before you began using electronics. How do your communication skills today compare with before you began using your electronics to communicate? Have they improved or diminished? If they have improved, is the improvement in all areas of communications? If your communications have not improved, how could you improve them?

*Interpreting Verbal and Nonverbal Cues*

Effective interpersonal communication also involves being able to read the body language and facial cues of the person receiving your information to note any signs of confusion, disagreement, or other reactions. When you're unable to determine how the information you are providing is being received, you are at a distinct disadvantage.

It's important to look for signs of confusion, which may involve the puzzled look on someone's face. This might entail the raising of one eyebrow and possibly the corner of his mouth turning up. Confusion or disagreement might also be demonstrated by someone sitting back and crossing his arms. Crossing of the arms can often be seen as an attempt to comfort one's self or to regain emotional equilibrium.

It's important to recognize the need to learn the full range of other's emotions to be able to accurately seek more information when it is necessary. Misreading someone can often happen, but the awareness that this is occurring is most important. In electronic communication, you really have no way of knowing whether the person is accurately receiving the information you are providing because the context is missing.

When was the last time you became offended or you insulted someone through electronic communication? Consider the lack of inflection, tone, and context electronic communication provides and the way this leads to miscommunication. What can you do to improve your interactions with others in your life?

## *Appropriate Use of Formal and Informal Language*

At times, it is important to recognize the need to be more formal in your communications. Amongst friends, it is very acceptable to speak using slang, jargon, and a vocabulary that is consistent with the culture and shared values. However, in more formal settings, it is important to recognize the need for clearer communication free of the elements of slang and jargon. If the individuals you are speaking to don't understand what you say, then you're not really communicating.

This often happens in groups at all levels of society. Professionals will often use the language of their profession but find that it alienates them when they begin communicating outside of their specialization. Individuals who use street language may find their choice of words foreign or even offensive to many individuals. It's important to consider who you are speaking to in considering the use of your language. Even the use of text language and e-speak can leave many individuals having to explain themselves or being completely misunderstood.

Remember, if you're not communicating so everyone understands you, you're not really communicating.

Consider how uncomfortable you would be in a group of highly specialized individuals using jargon specific to their job and specialty. Now consider how uncomfortable these same individuals would be surrounded by a group of texting teenagers speaking only in text speak. How does your use of language make those around you feel? If others don't understand you without explanations, then you are not really communicating.

*Effective Communication Is 100 Percent Your Responsibility*

It is generally understood that, if someone speaks, it is the responsibility of the person you are speaking to to ask for any clarifications needed. The problem is that the person you are speaking to may think she understands, but does she really? We cannot be sure that we communicate clearly, so it is often necessary to check in with the other person to make sure that what we said is clear and she understands what is said.

If there is any doubt, ask her to tell you what she heard you say. If what she tells you is not what you said, this gives you the opportunity to correct what she believes she heard. I also suggest that it is also 100 percent the responsibility of the person you are speaking to to ask for clarification if she thinks there is any possibility she is misunderstanding what you are saying.

It is also important that you let her know it is okay to ask if she has any questions. Therefore, communication is not a fifty-fifty proposition. Rather, communication is a 100 percent-100 percent equation in which both parties have responsibility.

Do you ever avoid face-to-face communications just to avoid dealing with others and life's issues? Is it embarrassing to clarify your understanding of each other face-to-face? If so, how do you propose making face-to-face communication as comfortable as electronic communication in order to effectively communicate?

## The Power of Self-Talk

Each of us engages in an internal, ongoing dialogue. It's your internal way of talking to yourself, thinking through your thoughts, making sense of your experiences, and communicating in the process of receiving information and expressing yourself. Your communication effectiveness depends on how accurately you interpret your experience. The accuracy of your interpretation can help you to achieve the results you are looking for or keep you from repeating failed patterns of behavior. It is important to develop and maintain your emotional and psychological health in order to accurately interpret and respond to the world around you. Overreliance on technology can provide inaccuracy in the interpretation of the surrounding world.

Generally, if your thoughts and expressions are counterproductive, friends or those truly caring about you may challenge you. This feedback can cause you to re-examine your positions and thoughts. However, in electronic communication, there is always someone online willing to support all kinds of unproductive and unhealthy perspectives, values, thoughts, and behaviors.

Without positive feedback and caring challenges to our behavior, we can stray into counterproductive and unhealthy behaviors. Those individuals who care about you and have your best interests in mind often challenge you to improve and grow. While this is often uncomfortable, it is essential to developing a healthy, balanced life.

When communicating online or in person, think to yourself, "Does this person have my best interest in mind?" If there is any doubt, be wary.

Those who love us and have our best interests in mind may challenge our way of thinking, even if only to ensure we are making the best and healthiest decisions possible. Do your online interactions/friends challenge you in any way to help you think more positively? If not, how do their interactions affect your life, either positively or negatively? Consider challenging your own way of thinking.

## Step #2: The Art of Social Conversation

*Being Interested vs. Being Interesting*

For some, social conversation appears to be as natural as getting hungry or rolling over in your sleep. For others, it can be a stressful and extremely uncomfortable situation. Often, not knowing how to engage others in conversation can lead to some of this discomfort. If you would like to feel more confident and capable in social settings, start getting interested in the lives of others, and you will often find that others are interested in you. This allows conversation and interpersonal interaction to become more natural.

Most people are interested in things that grab their awareness. And for many, what is most interesting is themselves. In starting conversations, become interested in those you speak to and learn to become a good listener. Listen for what is important to those you speak to. How do they see the world they live in? What (if anything) can you do, say, or provide them to help them to achieve something they want?

Notable speaker and business trainer, Zig Zigler, was known to say, "You can get all you want in life if you help enough other people get what they want."[63] It's been my experience that most individuals don't feel heard or validated. When you listen to them and can find value in what they say and want, you become a valued ally.

---

[63] "Zig Ziglar: 10 Quotes That Can Change Your Life," accessed June 12, 2013, *Forbes*. http://www.forbes.com/sites/kevinkruse/2012/11/28/zig-ziglar-10-quotes-that-can-change-your-life/

To become an improved conversationalist, become interested in the world around you. Watch the news, listen to different types of music, and discover varied pastimes. Pick up a magazine that you normally do not read and discover what others in different fields are looking at.

What makes others and you unique? Other people are often very interested in individuals who have a variety of experiences and lead interesting lives. Is your life boring? Become interested in the lives of others, and others are more likely to find you intriguing.

*Share the Conversation*

While it is important to be able to speak intelligently on different topics, it is even more vital to be able to listen well. It is essential to listen to what others are talking about and to learn to ask good questions. Cultivate an interest in true conversation. Develop the patience to allow the other person to fully explain himself before jumping in with a question.

Often when we are listening to others, we are so busy thinking of what we are going to say that we often miss much of their conversation. Practice suspending your thoughts and truly listening to them as they speak. This is not to say that others should dominate the conversation. But it is important in developing relationships to learn as much you can about the other person.

What people, places, things, or pets are central to their lives? What have they just experienced, or what are they currently going through? What are they looking forward to? Do they travel, and where do they find most interesting? It's often not very hard to find out a great deal of information about people if we really stop to listen to them.

## *Sharing Varied Experiences Yields Vibrant Conversation*

Often we tend to take our lives for granted, while others may find the things we do interesting and novel and would love to discuss them. What is unique to you? Have you had an experience in your past that allowed you to succeed in getting where you are today? Are you from a small town that no one has ever heard of? Do you have a hobby, skill, or passion that is unique or different that others might find of interest? There are often a number of experiences you had, places you have gone to, or people you have met that others would find fascinating.

## *Become Comfortable with Silence*

In conversation, it is not uncommon for a brief period of silence to occur. For many individuals, these periods of silence can be extremely uncomfortable and almost stressful. However, silence allows individuals to process their thoughts of what has been said and to further develop their options for carrying on the conversation.

It's amazing though how many people find even brief moments of silence unnerving. When they do feel uncomfortable, it is not uncommon for someone to try to fill the void. Yet giving someone a few moments to collect her thoughts in the midst of conversation can be very valuable to the development of your conversation.

Do silences or pauses in conversation make you uncomfortable? Next time you have a conversation, allow for natural pauses. How do they make you feel? How does it change the dynamic of the conversation for you as well as for the other person? What would happen if you asked the other person what she was thinking or feeling in the silence?

## Raise Options Rather Than Giving Opinions

Many individuals get into conversations as an opportunity to speak and work through their own thoughts. They may appear to be asking for help but may really be looking for someone they trust to be a sounding board.

My daughter called one day to share a series of concerns she had about a particular problem. I listened to her for several minutes and then attempted to solve the problem for her. She seemed to listen to what I was saying, but as she responded, she seemed a bit agitated. I then asked her if she would rather me simply listen and then provide answers, and she replied, "Yes, I really would!"

In our relationship, she often asks me for suggestions, but I also have to remember to ask her what she is looking for and not just assume she wants my help. As a parent of adult children, it is important for me to remember that I need to establish clear boundaries and to not overstep them. As children become adults, they have the right to make their own decisions, even if you may not agree.

As a parent of younger children, it was my responsibility to provide guidance and input on a regular basis even when kids didn't feel that they needed it. But now that they are adults, it is important to respect their experience, skills, knowledge, and wisdom. I'm still available if I can help them, but I can no longer assume they want me to solve their problems. It would be disrespectful for me to interject my opinions if they were unwanted.

The same is true with others in your life. Everyone has the right to her own thoughts, actions, and outcomes. To try to control any adult is to overstep your boundaries. It is not my job to run anyone else's life, and quite frankly, my hands are quite full with my own!

## Step #3: Making Relationships Work

*Making Friends*

With the increased frequency and volume of online dating, friendship development has been significantly transformed. However, because of the speed, intensity, and sometimes dismal results of online relationships, I think it's important to think about and develop real face-to-face, interpersonal relationships.

As mentioned before, the four Ts of true relationships are time, testing, tenacity, and triumph. Relationships developed over time have richness of experience and sharing that just seem to be enhanced the longer the relationship continues. Continued human interaction is essential for healthy development and relationship maintenance.

Another valuable aspect of interpersonal relationships is the testing that often takes place at the beginning and throughout the relationship that affirms each member's commitment to the relationship. Is he consistent over time so you can begin to trust what he says to be the truth, or does his commitment to the relationship fade over time when facing competing priorities and responsibilities?

Tenacity is the stick-to-it-ness that you find when people are with you through both the good and bad times. Anyone who has been in a long-term friendship or romantic relationship knows there are often disagreements and times of struggle in which misunderstandings and powerful feelings can occur. However, if there is enough commitment, respect, caring, and tenacity, then these relationships can endure over extended periods of time.

In all the years I have been married, my wife and I have often struggled because of our strong differences of opinion and the way we go about things. However, we both care deeply about each other, and we are committed to our relationship to the point where we are able to work through even some of the toughest problems life has thrown at us. We can't take each other for granted, and we seek to enhance the other person's life on a daily basis.

It's also important within any relationship to periodically celebrate the time spent together, the successes experienced, and the significant milestones achieved. I really believe we tend to forget the importance of celebration in our lives and may miss important benchmarks.

Inviting family and friends to take part in your achievements and significant events deepens those relationships and provides the "glue" that sustains us. Research even indicates that those individuals with strong social relationships tend to be healthier and happier than those who do not.[64]

How you celebrate the milestones in your relationships? How often? How do these celebrations contribute to or take away from the growth of your relationships? Is there anyone that you care about who would benefit from knowing you care about him, or what he has done in your life? Has anyone in your life made a significant contribution to your life that you would like to thank? Consider doing it now!

*Dating*

Online dating has significantly changed the way that people meet each other and develop relationships over time. Often these relationships develop faster with highly personal information shared more quickly, and engagement in physical intimacy happening at a far more rapid rate than prior to social networking and online relationships.

Students often begin a relationship online, carry it out online, and yet pass each other in the hall without speaking. And the first time they actually come together face-to-face is when they meet to have sex. They see no problem with establishing online relationships and having sex early in their interaction with the idea that, if the sex is good, only then will they continue to try developing a face-to-face relationship.

---

[64] This Emotional Life, "Intimate Relationships," accessed June 12, 2013, PBS. http://www.pbs.org/thisemotionallife/topic/relationships/intimate-relationships

There are several problems with this approach. First, online relationships do not prepare you for or encourage the development of skills necessary to carry on an ongoing interpersonal relationship. Many individuals who spend inordinate amounts of time online fail to develop or lose their ability to read facial cues and body language.

Individuals who have established interpersonal relationships find that they are able to continue and maintain their relationships online if need be. However, many individuals who find themselves establishing online relationships have difficulty once the relationship moves to an interpersonal level.

### *Dating Builds Best from Friendship*

Individuals often learn to develop common interests through shared experiences in the process of becoming friends. Friendships often blossom into more intimate relationships when based on the time individuals spend together, their ability to trust each other, their tenacity and dedication to the relationship, and commonly shared positive experiences.

This strong base of respect and commonality may result in deeper caring, which is often explored within a dating relationship. Without common respect and a degree of mutual needs being met within the bond, the relationship will often falter. However, a strong sense of friendship often provides the foundation for lasting relationships in addition to potential for greater intimacy.

*Resolving Conflict*

The most common problem I deal with when consulting organizations is the overreliance on text messaging and email. Conflicts sometimes result during the course of email and text messages because of the limited ability to truly communicate. Individuals will send a text or email that may be misinterpreted. When a response is returned that is inconsistent with the sender's intent, the sender often tries to correct the misinterpretation through another email. This results in a flurry of emails back and forth, each compounding the damage done in the previous correspondence.

Face-to-face communication is typically the best way to resolve any miscommunication. Face-to-face interactions provide the receiver with far greater information than mere black text on a white background. Resolving conflicts often demands upon both parties being committed to a resolution. This commitment is best demonstrated when one of the parties displays her willingness to take the first step. The first step can even be as simple as heading out of your office or cubicle to hers. If face-to-face interaction is not possible because of distance, talk to her on the phone.

Conflicts can be resolved when both parties commit to the development of a common vision. Expression of a common desired result often overrides any previous misconceptions and clarifies for both parties their interest in and willingness to achieve it. Establishing this common ground is difficult in an electronic communication because of the need to relate and empathize in the interaction.

*Working in Groups*

In a conversation with a manager from an internationally known Department of Defense missile defense company, I learned that they, like other companies, are having difficulty hiring individuals out of college who can effectively work in groups, communicate interpersonally, and brainstorm creatively in groups to find solutions. Working in groups requires multiple skills. It is important to be able to bond within a group because of expectation of acceptance and joining. Functional groups look for the value in existing and new members, recognizing the need for a healthy flow of people into a group to enhance its capacity and potential, to become more independent in order for them to grow in other ways. Healthy groups realize their potential by maximizing their members.

Individuals moving into groups need to strike a balance between the needs of the group and their own personal needs. Not only does finding a place and playing a role within the function of a group enhance the group, it gives a purpose to the individual within it. As individuals grow in their capacity, it is important for them to recognize their growth in relation to the organization.

At some point, an individual may grow in ways inconsistent with the needs of the group and may need to take a different role, join another group, or strike out on his own. When this happens, healthy organizations appreciate their members' contributions, celebrate their transition, and assist them in the process of moving out of the organization.

Functional groups develop a process for bringing in individuals, helping them in the transition, and providing continuing assistance and support. Functional organizations assimilate individuals into the larger membership by helping them define their roles and the way these roles relate to others in the group. This allows new members to strive toward a smooth introduction into the organization.

And when it is time for an individual to leave an organization, functional groups assist in his planning and transition and support him beyond his membership.

*Openness to Shared Thoughts*

In some cases, individuals have difficulty sharing their thoughts and allowing others to have input. They feel this is a personal affront, that their thoughts are their property and anyone building on them infringes on their rights to the original thought. When individuals lack boundaries or experience diminished ego, they may overreact when others are perceived as infringing upon their rights or diminishing them in some way.

Healthy individuals and organizations recognize the value of shared ideas. Diversity of experience, ideas, knowledge, and perceptions act like catalysts for exponentially benefiting everyone involved. How often are we annoyed when we see someone who has to be right? He may be dead wrong, but for some reason, he can't move from that position.

In the tech world, if you don't like someone or don't agree with his opinions, you can just "unfriend" him or leave the site or game he is in and seek a new group. Coming to a point where you can agree to disagree and move on is a valuable tool in your interpersonal skills toolbox.

In my work to create healthier-functioning individuals and organizations, there is often a hesitance to share success and failures. The benefit of sharing success is that, when you share success with others, you exponentially achieve more because "not one of us is as smart as all of us." When we help others to succeed, the experience lifts us up.

Explore your own personal and professional relationships. Do they display the four Ts relationships needed to succeed or otherwise allow you to move on and grow in and from them? If not, how are these relationships unhealthy and holding you back? People who care about you want you to succeed. Do those around you support your desire to be happy, healthy, and achieving what you want to achieve?

## Step #4: Self-Awareness (and Awareness of the Way You Express Your Emotions)

Reading others is a skill that can take years to develop. Only by interacting with others face-to-face can we really begin to get better at interpreting facial communications. You improve in the areas that you practice. So take the time to interact personally. Ask someone to lunch, join a club or organization to enhance your social life, and develop patience in the process.

By far, the majority of people I interact with are wonderful, giving, and caring individuals. But I would have never had the opportunity to get to know them if I had not taken the time, determined if I could trust them, stuck with it when we hit rough spots, and then enjoyed the company of the relationship as a result. Being in their presence helps us to connect on a more human level.

Real communication is more than words. It is the biological, psychological, and social connection we make when we enter the space of another human being. Sharing thoughts and words helps build understanding, but there is more to a relationship.

Do you know how others perceive you? Find someone you trust, and ask her to give you some feedback on how you come across. Remember that this is asking someone to take a huge risk in your relationship. If you really don't want to know or are not open to her honest feedback, then don't ask!

## Step #5: Living Skills

Many parents try to help their children by providing them everything they did not have. The only problem with this is that we often fail to realize we are who we are because of what we've gone through. Young people need to develop skills in their life that will serve them as adults.

One of these helpful skills is the ability to develop consistent habits, routines, and schedules. Having a consistent time to go to bed helps our bodies regulate and function more effectively. During adolescence, our biorhythms (or body clocks) run differently than when we are older. This means we need more rest, stay up later in the evening, sleep later in the morning, and may find it difficult to function in a nine-to-five society. Despite these difficulties, it's important for young people to develop some consistency in their lives while also allowing for the occasional weekend deviations to occur.

Young people need to accept responsibility for the environments they are in. Life skills like age-appropriate tasks around the house (for example, helping to picking up toys, bringing their clothes down to the laundry, and completing other small tasks) are good for young children. As they get older, insisting on daily tasks (for example, assisting with setting the table, doing dishes, learning to run the vacuum, and maintaining their own rooms) not only help them learn how to do these things but also teaches them responsibility within the family.

Educational responsibilities take precedent for high school students. However, at some level, responsibilities at home teach them to become dependable adults. It would not be unreasonable for them to assist in cleaning, mowing lawns, doing chores, or running errands.

They will need specific skills as adults that they can easily learn within the process of assisting around the house. Doing laundry, making phone calls to set up appointments, managing a checkbook, ordering food, and eating in public are all important life skills that cultivate responsible adults. It's amazing, but many young people I have encountered lack many of these rudimentary abilities because they were never encouraged to practice them while they were growing up.

Giving our children the resources, education, and skills they need to grow and succeed can be unsettling when they go off on their own and succeed beyond what we have been able to accomplish. It can be a blow to our ego or a challenge to our own sense of accomplishment. Remember that nothing says more about a teacher than to have a student go out and exceed them. Lifting others often means raising them beyond ourselves. Celebrate them and their successes. After all, they may be able to help you later on.

## Step #6: Establishing and Knowing Boundaries

It is important to understand and respect personal space whether during sessions of play as a child, in dating and developing friendships, or later in the work environment. Personal space is the distance and immediate surroundings that a person establishes to feel comfortable. Most Americans are comfortable with individuals approaching and speaking to them at arm's length. Touching others is often inappropriate unless it is in a handshake or otherwise invited. Personal objects of others should also be respected and left alone unless you are invited or given permission to touch them.

Yet, without practicing interactions in various settings, it may be difficult for some people to determine what is and is not appropriate. Parents can guide young children in the art of respecting the personal boundaries and property of others.

It can also be difficult for some individuals to know what and where to discuss certain subjects, which language to use, and where certain behaviors are inappropriate. It's important for parents to guide their children in knowing what is appropriate where. A lack of guidance from their parents can negatively impact a child's personal and social relationships.

Involving children in various social situations can provide the opportunity for coaching appropriate behavior. I've had parents tell me in the past that they often avoid these types of settings because it is easier than dealing with the poor behavior of their child. Yet dealing with behavior and coaching them will provide them with skills that they will need to use throughout their lives.

Being able to identify and react to social cues is an important aspect of effective social interaction. One such interpersonal skill is the art of knowing when others need to leave a conversation or end an interaction. It can be extremely frustrating for someone needing to leave a discussion to have the other person continually talking, completely unaware of the nonverbal communication.

Signals someone can give indicating that he needs to go can include some or all of the following: looking at a watch or clock; looking around the room, especially at the exit; packing up or gathering personal belongings; or simply turning away.

When these behaviors are noticed, it would be appropriate for the other person in the conversation to ask him if he needs to leave. This can allow the person listening to say he does or does not. It's important to be aware of nonverbal communication because it can often make the other person feel awkward if you don't care or can't convey the sense that you do.

Boundaries are also vital in the use of the Internet and social media. Consider the information you put up there. It's there forever. Post information as if you were posting it on the front page of your local newspaper or highway billboard. Others don't need to know your latest mistake, video of criminal activity, the problems with your latest flame or spouse, and the medication you or someone in your family is on.

I am constantly amazed with the amount of information posted on social networking sites. Keep your views of your job private unless they are the best in the world to work for. If anyone is involved in health care, posting information that identifies a client or patient is a violation of privacy, and legal actions can result. Most employers, future dates, lawyers, and the courts regularly search the web for information that is often readily available. Parents need to teach and monitor the information posted on the Internet. And most of all, model the type of behavior they want to see in their children.

Consider your own boundaries both in the real world as well as on the Internet. Are they inappropriate or otherwise compromised? What impact does this have on your life outside of the virtual world? Would you be willing to post all you do on social networking sites on a billboard along the main street in your community?

## Step #7: The Art of Relaxation

Many individuals don't know what to do when there is nothing to do. This goes for young people as well as adults. Being able to comfort yourself and be relaxed is a skill well worth learning. Leading a balanced life requires involvement in a variety of activities and responsibilities, of which there are three basic categories that should be addressed: physical responsibilities, psychological health responsibilities, and social responsibilities.

### *Physical Responsibilities*

Physical responsibilities include those of your family— children included—to eat properly, get enough rest as well as exercise, and maintain a healthy approach to life. The stresses of life and the stress we put on ourselves through work and the use of technology can take its toll on us over time.

Relaxation techniques can include leisure recreation, reading books, engaging in arts and crafts, prayer, and meditation. These meditative activities can help offset much of the stressors in our lives. Additionally, when combined with physical activity, not only do you offset the negative effects, you create positive results of increased circulation, improved muscle tone, enhanced oxygenation of our bodies, and improved overall health. You will likely sleep better and may find yourself having more energy.

The combination of an active lifestyle and periods of relaxation can greatly enhance your life and the life of your children. Consider modeling these behaviors so your kids can see that it works in the lives of their parents. You may be one of the best models of success they could possibly have, so be what you want to see in them.

*Psychological Responsibilities*

The second responsibility is to your and your children's psychological health. Like your physical health, your psychological health also needs to be maintained. It is often easy to see when our physical health declines, but it is often more difficult to identify when our or our children's psychological health declines.

Learning new information from a variety of sources continues to expand your potential and your outlook on life. Having individuals in your life who are healthy, functional, and positive provides support when it is needed. Spending time in the presence of positive people can inspire and enlighten us and help maintain a more positive outlook. Entertaining different points of view challenges us in our thinking and keeps us from mentally stagnating. When this is combined with goal setting and continued personal growth, greater personal fulfillment often results.

It's also important for us to recognize when things in our lives are not working properly and to seek support and assistance when it is needed. It is always amazing to me that physical ailments occur and we have no problem going to a doctor or hospital to address them. Yet when we are confronted with any type of psychological ailment (from recent loss to depression to uncontrolled anger), we often ignore, rationalize, or deny it.

Mental health is just as important as physical health in needs to be maintained. And quite honestly, I believe almost everyone would benefit from a periodic checkup from the neck up. If you see a problem, a change in behavior, or any of the indicators listed above, get help immediately. The last thing anyone can afford is denial. Mental health issues often go unaddressed because we don't know what to do.

## Social Responsibilities

In addition to our responsibilities of physical and physiological health, we have a third responsibility that includes our social interactions because no one lives in a vacuum. Over the past several years, research studies consistently shows that individuals who have a strong and healthy social support system tend to live longer and lead happier lives.

Being a part of a family or an organization in the community gives us security and a sense of balance through which we maintain a healthier perspective on our world. Children who are exposed, coached, and encouraged to make and maintain social interactions learn a whole host of skills and capabilities that we've covered throughout this manual. The opportunity to experience a wide range of social interactions provides a greater context for learning to read and succeed in all of your relationships.

Many individuals find work, hobbies, and other activities very relaxing. But how? Those who find certain activities extremely relaxing generally also find that these activities create a sense of flow for them. Flow is a state of mind and body where time can either stand still or seem to pass very rapidly. In flow states, we actually relax by putting all of our effort, attention, and energy into a singular task we are involved in.

With technology use, the hypnotic interactions with the computer create flow states. However, in our tasks and activities, flow states are achieved by learning to focus our attention, applying patience in mobilizing our energies into the task at hand, and expending effort for the sole purpose of completing the task. In this manner, we are doing the activity for ourselves.

Learning to achieve flow states can be highly beneficial for the enjoyment and satisfaction of the activity. This is a very different type of experience because the skills that are developed can serve you in the long term. For children diligently staying with the task, being able to concentrate, applying their efforts, and seeing positive results forms a pattern of behavior that enables them to achieve flow states over time.

Being a part of a social interaction also comes with some responsibility to those you interact with. In social networking, individuals often seek assistance online. This presents the opportunity for parents and other caretakers to discuss with their children and young adults the dangers of putting too much information online and sharing family business with strangers, as well as being careful not to put too much trust into the guidance and recommendations you get online. The family is a vital social structure that needs constant maintenance. Talk with those in your family about things that matter in their lives. Spend time away from technology in order to check in and find out how others are doing. It would be sad to spend more time interacting and more involvement in those beyond the walls of our homes than we do with our own families. Yet many individuals today report this is not uncommon.

How are you physically, emotionally, and socially? Do any of these areas need a checkup? Consider the repercussions of technology use on each area of your life, and if it is out of balance, take action now!

## Step #8: Creative Thought

When skills are combined with better tools in your toolbox, improved results can be expected. Unfortunately, creativity and exploration are two areas in danger today.

Much of our entertainment is delivered directly to us without any need for us to think for ourselves. This can make our thinking and creative processes fat and lazy, limiting our ingenuity and reducing our ability to problem-solve. Freeing your mind is both a liberating and empowering undertaking. Yet how do we do it?

Children are born exploring. Watching a newborn searching for a finger to suck on or a young child spending periods of time with a box is an exhilarating experience. Not only is this essential for our growth, it is stimulating to our ability to maintain a youthful outlook on life. My belief is, to quote George Bernard Shaw, "We don't stop playing when we get old, we get old when we stop playing."[65]

Many children today spend far too much time in front of a television or computer not learning or developing the skills necessary to effectively problem-solve, create, and play. Play can be serious business, yet with today's electronic toys, much of the imagination has been taken out of the play.

I suggest that young children avoid the use of electronic video games and instead be given blocks, cardboard boxes, simple stuffed animals, and other plastic toys that require imagination and creativity to be brought to life. As parents, it's important to spend time showing them how to play. And if you don't know how to play, learn. Numerous programs at hospitals and early childhood centers will teach parents how to interact with their young children.

Take them outside. Let them explore the grass, trees, bushes, and sounds of nature. Go fishing, rent a canoe, or just go for a hike. These will all increase your opportunities to model healthy behavior, enhance your physical interaction with your child, and talk in an unstructured setting. Some of the best conversations I've ever had with my kids were when we were building sand castles, canoeing, or gardening together in our front yard.

Go with older kids to a ballgame or listen to their band play. Find out what they're interested in and get involved in it with them. Ask them questions about what they think. And make sure you are willing to listen without judgment.

---

[65] BrainyQuotes, accessed June 12, 2013. http://www.brainyquote.com/quotes/quotes/g/georgebern120971.html

Often we are more willing to think freely in a safe, secure, and predictable environment. Expansive thinking occurs best in a safe place, where we can share our thoughts without fear of reprisal, ridicule, or feeling stupid. As parents, it's important to correct and give guidance, but it is also important to create a safe enough physical and psychological space for children and young people to grow creatively.

By providing them with opportunities to explore their thoughts, actions, reactions, and dreams, they are able to create and develop far greater options in thinking and behavior. I believe the parent's job is to encourage their diversity of thought, expand the possibilities for compliment, and nurture their utilization of these various skills to achieve everything they are capable of achieving.

Young people and adults can get caught in the trap of trying to be perfect when we actually want to see simple progress. The achievement of success relative to your own ability, not the attainment of perfection, measures progress. If you create and attain the highest level you personally are capable of, then you are truly successful.

Do you know how to engage in imaginative play? Take time away from technology to engage in something your mind must manipulate in order to enjoy whether with a young child or as if you are one. How does this play/interaction differ from its virtual counterpart? Consider letting young people in on solving household problems. You might be surprised at their ability to creatively problem-solve. You just might learn something together in the process!

## Step #9: Managing Emotions

Being able to manage one's emotions is a valuable tool for the effective management of life. Children and adults benefit greatly from understanding that they don't need to simply react to everything around them. They can take time to analyze the circumstances, decide on a variety of options, and then choose which of those options best meets their needs. They can decide to completely ignore any circumstance, choosing instead to go about their business as if nothing had happened.

Or they may decide to find humor, irony, or surprise in whatever circumstance they're in. They may choose to become angry. At which point, they have a variety of options, including the realization that there might be nothing they can do to change the circumstance.

They may acknowledge the anger and take appropriate action to resolve a wrongdoing, or they may express their anger, recognizing it is an emotion that they feel needs to come out instead of being bottled up. When anger is ignored or denied, it can turn to resentment, the unhealthy harboring of anger turned inward, potentially resulting in depression, self-harm, or other inappropriate expressions.

An important concept to remember in dealing with emotions is the fact that they do not necessarily have to dictate the actions you take. Just because you feel an emotion doesn't mean you have to act on it. In each circumstance, as previously described, there are a variety of options regarding how to react. It is important to recognize the need for appropriate responses so your actions relieve the anger or resentment you feel while also effectively expressing, correcting, or releasing the resulting emotions.

Taking time to think before you react allows you to distance yourself from any reaction you may have. Thinking before speaking reduces your tendency to overreact and allows your rational side to more effectively respond to the circumstances.

In managing your emotions, it is also important to own your ideas with I statements like, "When you said_____, I felt_____ ." This approach is far better than blaming or name-calling as a result of your emotions. Once you state how you felt in relation to what the person did or said, you are able to let the other person know how her behavior had an impact on you.

The difficulty here is that very often there is an expectation that other people will immediately change as a result. Once you have said how you felt in relation to their actions, it's important to step back and recognize that it is up to them to decide how they will react to this information. Your responsibility in managing and appropriately sharing your emotions is not to make someone else do something, but to appropriately express yourself in relating your understanding of how their behavior impacted you. After sharing how you feel, it is also important for you to let it go and move on. You can use this in expressing both positive and negative feelings you experience.

Interpersonal relationships can provide you with opportunities to learn a great deal about yourself. So pay attention to when your emotions rise because these situations can provide insights to what triggers your own behavior.

Your job in this world is not to change other people but to understand yourself with greater clarity so you can effectively respond to the world around you, all the while helping to meet your needs and the needs of others.

Technology today is so reactive that the skills of patience, responding rather than merely reacting, paying attention to, and managing our emotions, all seem to be greatly diminished. As a result, many in today's technology age report to me that they feel they have to quickly react to their surrounding circumstances instead of taking the time to think and generate options for their actions.

How does your technology use affect your interactions with others? Are you thoughtful in the response to your emotions, or do you simply react? Consider technology's role in your reaction. Is the choice you are making the best choice at this time and in this situation? What other options are available? What will happen if you choose not to respond? What will happen if you do? Take the time to explore your options. Life is not always right or wrong!

## Step #10: Getting a Life

For many social workers today, it's not uncommon to go into homes where there is very little food, inadequate clothing, and a significant lack of resources, but yet there is often a large-screen television, pricey computer, and high-end cell phones. After seeing this for the past couple years, I have come to believe that TV, computers, and phones provide access to an alternative life outside the experience of interpersonal struggles, family problems, poverty, unfulfilled needs, and deprivation.

For many, technology provides an opportunity to escape the hardships of their life, to virtually travel to places they would never otherwise see, to become anyone they want to be. The Internet is therefore said to be a great equalizer, that is, it provides everything to everyone. But does it?

For many, technology today provides a portal for disconnecting from themselves, not only their world. In spite of extreme personal struggles, family problems, or more than adequate resources and tremendous potential, they enter this portal, losing themself in the process. And the scary thing about it is that it often happens so subtly that they don't notice that it is happening.

But what can we do about this disconnection for real life? Here are six things that you can do today to help you become more connected to the real life that you actually live:

- Begin to chart how much time you spend without conversation, watching TV, spending time on the computer, and using your cell phone versus how much time you spend interacting with family and friends.
- Commit to equalizing the amount of time you spend using technology recreationally and in social networks versus the face-to-face time spent with family and friends.
- Take twenty minutes each day for physical exercise, along with twenty minutes each day for a period of silence, prayer, or mediation.
- Every night before you go to bed, begin to write down all the good things that happened in your life that day. Even if it is only one or two things, write them down, and keep the list.

- Make a list each morning of three things you plan to achieve that day. If you have more than three, make a separate list and put it into your desk drawer. Once the first three have been accomplished, cross them off, and add three more to your list. But only keep three active items in front of you at one time.
- Commit to playing in any non-tech form for one hour at least three times per week.

Computers are wonderful tools that can make our lives more productive, enhance our creativity, and allow us to experience life in new and fascinating ways. The world with all of its intellectual riches is now at our fingertips. It is up to us to use it for our betterment or detriment.

I only hope that we remember that the most amazing computing organism that exists and may ever exist is the one we were given at birth that resides between our ears. I hope we don't abandon it, chasing the marvels of marketing in which we are limited. The mind is only now beginning to be understood. The limits of the mind are yet to be determined and may yet prove to be the seat of the soul. Only time will tell.

# Epilogue: What now?

Most people get a fair amount of fun out of their lives, but on balance life is suffering, and only the very young or the very foolish imagine otherwise.[66]

—George Orwell

I truly began to live when I discovered that honest effort, sustained struggle, and, at times, pain were a part of life. I tried avoiding, evading, and finding newer and more improved ways to live struggle free, but they just didn't work. Just when a new approach, strategy, tool, or toy came along, it promised to improve my life so I didn't have to work so hard, deal with myself, struggle with frustration, or all of the other things I'd try to avoid in life. I'd then discover they just didn't work. Is this what we try to do today through the magic of technology? Faster, smarter, easier, and immediate is not always the best way.

There are benefits to discovering frustration, tolerance, patience, and an understanding of ourselves and others. Technology has made a positive difference in our lives, but it is not a replacement for learning to live life on life's terms. Avoiding interactions and finding ways to not deal with people and social

[66] Ibid. http://www.brainyquote.com/quotes/quotes/g/georgeorwe159442.html

151

interaction only delays the inevitable. We all deal with others, and those who do it well seem to find more satisfaction in the relationships they have.

Those seeking a softer and easier way may advance in some areas of life but may also miss out on the broad spectrum of experiences life has to offer. Like a piece of coal, these high pressure life experiences teach, cleanse, and change us into the diamonds we have the potential of becoming. Through life's challenges, our minds are tempered, our bodies toughened, and our spirits honed to form the foundation of skills and experience upon which a greater appreciation of life resides. Balance in life comes at a cost, yet the dividends realized are exponentially greater for those willing to fully experience all that life has to offer.

I encourage you to utilize all that technology has to offer if it makes your life more productive, your relationships more meaningful, and your mind work faster. But find balance in your life. Go outside, strike up a conversation, explore your environment, learn an art, travel and experience new things, strengthen your body, find your upper levels of ability, and then be still to discover the inner space of your mind as you explore a region far more vast than the far reaches of space. Love someone enough to discover his flaws, and love him anyway. You were put here for a reason that is totally unique to you. Find out what it is! Life is far too short than to be limited to only the world encapsulated within anything operated by an on/off switch. Turn off, and tune in!

Be well!
John

*The Pond: A Small Book about Making Big Changes*
John K. Kriger

When a community of animals living in a once peaceful, stable pond find themselves confronted with the awareness of an ever-changing world, they become afraid, indecisive, panicky, and quarrelsome. They soon realize that only when they are willing to undertake reasonable risks and consider changing their thinking are their individual and organizational capabilities awakened. The animals soon learn that new thinking brings about new and positive results, making the process of change empowering and exciting.

Change in organizations, whether in the workplace, community groups, or even in family life, is inevitable. While some welcome change and thrive on the opportunities it presents, many find it difficult to move ahead, imagining the worst along a road filled with insurmountable risk. Change management can be a challenge even for those with experience, as each case is unique.

But for managers, leaders, human resource professionals, and anyone seeking tools for themselves and their teams, the story of *The Pond* provides insights and tools to assist in maintaining a "pristine pond" or in transforming a "stagnant swamp." Change can be successful when there is hope in the midst of uncertainty. Through learning how to look at things anew, you can truly awaken your potential.

Author's discount and volume pricing available at www.krigerconsulting.com.

< http://www.krigerconsulting.com/resources.html>

# Suggested Readings

Brodie, Richard. *Virus of the Mind: The New Science of the Meme.*
Seattle: Integral, 1996.

Cash, Hilarie, and Kim McDaniel. *Video Games & Your Kids:
How Parent Stay in Control.* Enumclaw: Idyll Arbor, 2008.

Doidge, Norman. *The Brain That Changes Itself: Stories of Personal
Triumph from the Frontiers of Brain Science.* New York: Viking,
2007.

Heath, Chip, and Dan Heath. *Made to Stick: Why Some Ideas
Survive and Others Die.* New York: Random House, 2007.

Jensen, Eric. *Brain-based Learning: The New Paradigm of Teaching.*
Thousand Oaks: Corwin, 2008.

Kotulak, Ronald. *Inside the Brain: Revolutionary Discoveries of
How the Mind Works.* Kansas City: Andrews and McMeel,
1996.

Medina, John, Mark Pearson, and Richard W. Stevenson. *Brain
Rules: 12 Principles for Surviving and Thriving at Work, Home,
and School.* Seattle: Pear, 2008.

Pink, Daniel H. *A Whole New Mind: Why Right-Brainers Will Rule
the Future.* New York: Riverhead, 2006.

Schwartz, Jeffrey, and Sharon Begley. *The Mind and the Brain:
Neuroplasticity and the Power of Mental Force.* New York:
Regan /HarperCollins Publ., 2002.

Small, Gary W., and Gigi Vorgan. *IBrain: Surviving the Technological Alteration of the Modern Mind*. New York: Collins Living, 2008.

Struthers, William M. *Wired for Intimacy: How Pornography Hijacks the Male Brain*. IVP Books, 2009.

Young, Kimberly S. *Internet Addiction: A Handbook and Guide to the Evaluation and Treatment*. Honoken: John Wiley & Sons, 2011.

# About the Author

For over twenty-five years, John has consistently evolved as a person, national and international speaker, and recognized expert on organizational leadership and technology dependence, developing and delivering engaging presentations worldwide. As president of Kriger Consulting, Inc., he has worked with hundreds of organizations and thousands of individuals to create healthier and more functional individuals, communities, and workplaces.

John has received numerous awards for his work in prevention and his service to various communities. In addition, John is also author of *The Pond: A Small Book about Making Big Changes*. This manuscript, *Turned On & Tuned Out*, is a practical guide to understanding and managing technology dependence, and he is completing his newest book on *The Art of Prezentation*.

He holds a bachelor's degree in human services and a master's degree in management, and he is a Licensed Clinical Alcoholism and Drug Abuse Counselor. Additionally, John is a nationally Certified Prevention Specialist, a member and past board member of the National Speakers Association, as well as a member of the International Speakers Network. He is a frequent lecturer at various colleges and universities, including Rutgers University and Stockton College, and he is a visiting professor at Beijing Normal University in China.

CPSIA information can be obtained
at www.ICGtesting.com
Printed in the USA
FFHW022244021118
49246084-53460FF